Scale

CONSTRUCTION

Scale
CONSTRUCTION

BY DUNCAN HUTSON

Published by Traplet Publications Limited 1996
Traplet House,
Severn Drive,
Upton-upon-Severn,
Worcestershire. WR8 0JL
United Kingdom.

Reprinted in 1999

ISBN 1 900371 05 7

Front Cover
Close up study of the author's Hanriot HD-1.

Back Cover
Scale construction detail of the author's SE5A.

Printed and bound by Stephens & George Limited,
Merthyr Industrial Estate, Dowlais, Merthyr Tydfil, Mid Glamorgan CF48 2TD

About the Author

1974 saw the launch of the scale plans range from Duncan Hutson, the first of which was the Britten Norman Islander. Many other successful designs followed which included his 112" span Fournier RF5 that he took to the 1980 World Championships in Canada where he was the highest placed British team member.

In 1996 he entered the Tiger Moth in the Large Scale event at the World Championships in France achieving the highest static score and coming 2nd overall.

In 1989 Duncan ventured into the kits market creating accurate, true scale models. These proved very successful in competitions with the prototype Tiger Moth kit winning the 1992 and 1996 British Nationals and also placing well in many other competitions.

As well as building first class models Duncan has been the regular Scale Flyer columnist for R/C Model World since 1985, covering all major scale meetings and giving tips on how to build better scale models.

Recently Duncan decided to concentrate only on scale kits and the scale plans along with the glassfibre cowls, canopies, etc. are now being handled through R/C Model World (Traplet Publications). However, Duncan's scale kits are still available direct from Duncan at 33 Hartlebury Way, Charlton Kings, Cheltenham, Gloucestershire, GL52 6YB.

Contents

Introduction

Radio controlled scale models – why should anyone want to make them when they are more complicated to build and less practical than the sport model equivalent. Comments such as this are brandished around from time to time at the club flying site, generally by those who have had little experience of scale modelling. True these comments were probably quite accurate twenty years ago – maybe even ten years ago they weren't too far from the truth. In recent years, however, there has been a great improvement in the reliability of the radio control equipment that we now take so much for granted. There has also been great strides in the complexity of radios which is certainly an advantage when controlling the more sophisticated scale model.

The other area of improvement for reliability has been the introduction and development of the four stroke glow motor. Although the two stroke is cheaper and more powerful for its size and weight, it nevertheless doesn't have the realistic sound of the four stroke. These big improvements in the performance of radios and engines have now meant that the scale modeller's attention can be devoted to building and flying the model rather than trying to keep his radio or engine working reliably which was the problem in previous years.

To the sceptic who still feels that scale modelling isn't worth the effort I must say that, from my admittedly "biased standpoint", I feel that it is the ultimate challenge in modelling. I am sure that when you have had a look at a fullsize airfield you will have noticed that all the aircraft look a lot like larger versions of scale models! To me, the challenges involved in creating a miniature version of some fullsize counterpart can be a very gripping and absorbing hobby indeed.

The final proof that you have been successful comes

The author's 1/4 scale De Havilland Tiger Moth with Tony Bull's version of the same aircraft shows the diversity of colour schemes even with the same prototype.

The uncovered airframe of the author's Hanriot HD-1 reveals the internal structure of this model.

on the day when your latest creation takes to the air for the first time and flies satisfactorily. Indeed there can be few greater pleasures in life than the test flight of a model which performs successfully but the satisfaction I find is in proportion to the amount of effort I have put into designing and building the model.

The challenges of radio controlled scale modelling are numerous, the two most obvious being the indoor aspect of building and all that this can entail with the outdoor sport element of flying the aircraft. There are many modellers who excel in one particular area but are fairly weak in the other aspect though there are undeniably some who seem to excel in both, particularly on the competition circuit.

My fascination for modelling in its various shapes and forms started many, many years ago when I was just big enough to pick up a clockwork train. I subsequently progressed from clockwork through to electric trains through to model boats with a small amount of radio control as that is all the valve radios of those days would allow (if you could keep them working that is). With the introduction of transistor radios, I learnt to fly proportional radio control in sport and aerobatic models and developed my flying skills that way.

Many crashes later (through inexperience and the lack of reliability of some of the earlier radios) I still had a desire to move to the more rewarding sphere of scale modelling. Although there were some scale plans and kits available at that time the choice was very limited

indeed although I did build from one or two scale plans of the time. It was not long before I felt the urge to design my own scale models and the satisfaction and reward that was to give me over the years. Having now designed more than twenty different scale models and built many more over the time I see no reason for stopping now and will go on for many years yet.

Chapter 1

Where to Start in Scale

I have often been asked the question by those considering taking up radio control model aircraft flying as to what type of scale model one should start with. Perhaps a little clarification here might be a good idea as, if you have had no experience of radio control flying, scale may not be your best starting point.

The reasons are fairly obvious when you look at them as it takes a little more effort to build a scale model than it would a quick build kit high wing trainer type model. The trainer model will also have been designed to be easy to build and, more to the point, easy and stable to fly. Although flying a model aircraft is not particularly difficult there are some basic skills which can take a little while to become proficient at. One of the biggest problems can be when the aircraft is flying towards you since right is no longer right and to react quickly can take a great deal of practice and time.

Learning to land a model aircraft needs practice as you need to start the landing approach in the right part of the sky if you hope to make contact with the ground in the appropriate place and, hopefully, in the right attitude as well! Also building a trainer type model will give you some of the basic building skills required which you will need to perfect if you are to build a scale model successfully.

Once one has learnt to fly proficiently on a high wing stable aircraft then it is logical to move to a low wing aircraft which is naturally less stable but more responsive and will also have ailerons as the primary control for roll and turn where the high wing model may well have only rudder for turning. This sort of model will be good practice to get your responses to an automatic level and enable you to try out aerobatic manoeuvres as well. The other advantage is that if you make a mistake flying this type of model and contact terra firma in an unscheduled way it shouldn't be the end of world to rebuild the model and get it back in the air once more. With a scale model, repairs and accidents are more costly exercises in both time and money.

Once flying a model has become an easy exercise and you need only concentrate on positioning the manoeuvres now could well be the logical time to start building your first scale model. Even if you feel that you are a confident flier it still does no harm to select a basically stable aircraft as this will give you confidence when the time comes to to fly the model. Such aircraft as Piper Cubs – which are high wing and inherently stable with good flying characteristics – make an ideal obvious first choice. An aircraft I built a number of years ago which falls into a similar category is the Luton Minor which, in its fullsize form, is an English homebuilt aircraft and is powered either by a Jap 35hp motor or a 1200 Volkswagen car engine suitably adapted for aircraft use of course. My model was 62" span and 40ci powered with 4-channel radio.

A number of bi-planes can be very easy to fly and stable aircraft – certainly the larger ones are quite forgiving in their characteristics.

The other question you might well ask is whether your first scale model should be fairly large or fairly small. Obviously if it is fairly small then it will be cheaper to build, require a smaller and therefore less expensive motor to power it, and be easier to transport in your car to the flying site. The obvious disadvantages of a

A pack of Piper Cubs make a colourful scale model but more importantly a good stable flying aircraft.

This 1/3 scale Durine Turbulent is also a forgiving aircraft to fly with a wide undercarriage as well.

small aircraft are that the weight can build up quite easily and it can become heavy for its size or have a higher wing loading than is ideal for a first scale model.

These days, with the improvements in radios and engines that I have already mentioned, the general trend has moved to somewhat larger models which have several advantages. Firstly their size makes them easier to see at a distance and therefore easier for the pilot to control which can be quite a large plus for the inexperienced pilot. Also having a larger wing area the weight of the model will be less of a problem, as such items as the radio will remain the same whether it is in a large or small aircraft apart from possibly an increase in the num-

ber of servos. There is also another advantage and without getting bogged down in technical aerodynamic terms, the simple fact is that a larger wing cord is more efficient than its smaller counterpart, a situation that exists in fullsize aerodynamics as well.

There are many modellers who want to build a Spitfire as their first scale model and perhaps wonders why it was slightly less successful than they hoped it would be. First of all the Spitfire is a low wing aircraft equipped with ailerons which makes it inherently less stable. It also has a retracting undercarriage which is an extra technical element to add to the building side of it and if one is not that experienced they can be a little tricky to fit and get working reliably even using the best of the commercial systems available these days. As the prototype had a liquid cooled engine and if the model engine is to be kept out of sight within the fuselage, cooling your model engine will present a problem and can lead to a lack of reliability. On the aerodynamic side the tailplane tends to be rather on the small side for ideal model dimensions coupled with the elliptical tapered wing which makes the aircraft potentially not too stable. All of this can make for slightly difficult flying characteristics.

The Spitfire makes a very attractive and exciting scale model to fly. The elliptical tapered wing is difficult to build coupled with the retracting undercarriage and small tailplane and is not recommended as your first or even second scale model.

As we are trying to select a type of aircraft that is suitable for your first one or two scale models a Spitfire and aircraft of a similar background do not generally lend themselves to being good first scale models. On the other hand I will admit to having seen a number built over the years by experienced scale builders and fliers which have obviously been very exciting aircraft to fly and have looked very impressive indeed.

FU4 Corsair has a twist and turn retracting undercarriage and retracting tailwheel. These are difficult items to make reliably coupled with the bent wing which is also difficult to build. This is yet again not a beginners aircraft but with experience can be a superb flying model in the hands of someone like Brian Taylor.

There used to be an amusing story going around the competition circuit of a young lad who went into the model shop and wanted to buy a large lump of balsa wood to carve into the shape of a Lancaster and stick four engines on it. When the model shop proprietor was asked whether this was a suitable project for his first aircraft, the proprietor said that he didn't really think so!

Multi-engined aircraft can be a very challenging and rewarding section of this hobby which I have personally enjoyed myself having built no less than six twin-engined aircraft over the years. Knowing how to set up engines and getting them to be completely reliable is very much a part of multi-engine flying and this is something which is only gained by experience.

There are a number of American light aircraft such as this one which has very attractive colour schemes and would make an ideal first scale model.

The Fly Baby is a good forgiving scale model and would certainly be an ideal first low wing aircraft.

I hope that, if you were thinking of starting on a WW2 fighter as your first scale model, I haven't depressed you too much but unfortunately the information I have given is based on experiences I have seen, other people suffer the same experiences which has not always led to too much success.

It is always a good idea to model an aircraft which you like and have a lot of enthusiasm for. Although I have suggested such an aircraft as a Piper Cub for a scale model if you personally cannot stand the sight of it you are unlikely to have any success or enthusiasm with the project and therefore it is potentially doomed to failure. What I have tried to suggest is the type of aircraft which would make a suitable first choice before you venture onto the potentially more exciting and challenging projects. It is in fact a good idea to progress steadily through various stages and types of aircraft following a fairly logical sequence.

I have seen people come into the hobby with a great deal of enthusiasm and try to advance too quickly and the result has been some unfortunate crashes at which point they have decided that the hobby wasn't worth the effort and, sadly, left it with an unpleasant taste in their mouth. If they had been given better advice at the beginning they might well still be in the hobby and reaping the rewards.

Building A Scale Model

Would-be scale modellers often ask whether they should build from a plan or buy a commercial kit or even perhaps design their own. The latter option is very simple to answer – you should not attempt designing your own models until you have built and flown quite a few scale models successfully.

These days there are a wide selection of scale plans and most of the designers offer glassfibre cowls and vac-formed canopies which are two of the hard parts to make on a one-off basis. You will have to select your own wood, cut all the parts and assemble the aircraft working purely from the information on the plan. The obviously advantages are that it may be cheaper – it certainly enables you to spread the expenditure over a longer period. Building from a plan will assume that you have basically good woodworking skills, reasonable workshop facilities and the space and time to do it.

Kit building means that a lot of the hard work has already been done for you. In a kit one would expect all the wing ribs to be die-cut or CNC cut, fuselage formers pre-cut to shape, so really there should not be a lot more than an assembly job to build the model completely. Some scale aircraft kits will have a very comprehensive list of scale accessories whilst others will leave you to go down to your local model shop and try and obtain the necessary parts. Each scale plans designer or kit manufacturer will approach the designing of a model in his own way and if you find that you like the products of one particular manufacturer you may well decide to stick with them in the future.

If you have built a trainer model it will probably have had a foam core and veneered wing which made for a very quick build model. These are sometimes used on scale models but generally, because of their limitations particularly when fitting retracting undercarriages or flaps, they are not popular. They can be used on some of the very simple scale kits that are not 100% accurate. Most scale models will feature pre-cut wing ribs and what is called traditional built-up construction.

The author's Miles Gemini twin was an absorbing project to build yet fraught with problems at the flying site. In this landing shot you can see that the starboard engine has stopped. Even in experienced hands this can be a problem. Twins should not be an early challenge in your scale modelling career.

Chapter 2

Scale Wings Construction

It would seem logical to start with the subject of building wings because if it doesn't have wings it's not an aircraft!

If you have bought a kit which contains a pair of foam wings they will certainly need joining in the middle. First of all check the fit of the wings in the middle to make sure that you have the correct dihedral under each tip. To join the wings it is a good idea if you mix up some five minute epoxy and apply it to the edge of the joint around the veneer. The wings can be pressed together with the tips supported to allow the epoxy to set. This has the advantage of holding the wings in the correct position and also seals the joint when you are applying the glassfibre bandage. If you are applying the bandage with polyester resins and this comes in contact with the foam cores the resin will dissolve the foam with disastrous consequences. The five minute epoxy joining the veneers will stop the polyester resin getting to the foam which is important. If on the other hand you are using epoxy resins to secure the glassfibre bandage then there is no problem since it will not dissolve the foam cores. Sticking the two cores together will make it much simpler when you apply the 6" wide glassfibre bandage as you will be able to go around the top and bottom of the wing in one go. Since the glassfibre will contribute a lot to the strength of the wings in this very important area the only type you should use is the woven cloth which will usually come from a roll which is around 6" wide. The cheaper, chopped mat glassfibre will break in this application very quickly and cause the wings to fail in flight!

When the glassfibre has had an adequate time to properly set you will need to blend it into the veneer surface of the wings. If you try rubbing the edge of the glassfibre down there is a great risk that you will also sand away some of the veneer which will greatly weaken the wings near the centre of the model. Fig.1 illustrates this point.

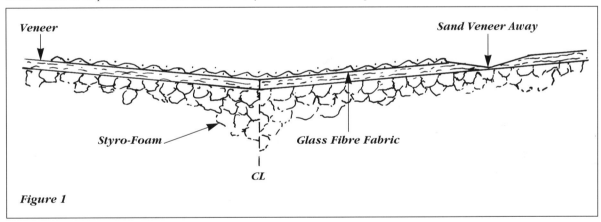

Figure 1

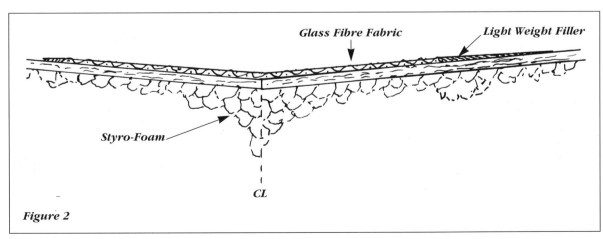

Figure 2

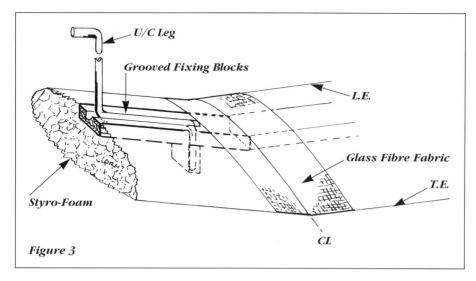

Figure 3

Labels in figure: U/C Leg, Grooved Fixing Blocks, L.E., Glass Fibre Fabric, T.E., Styro-Foam, CL

during the manufacturing stage of the wing. There are basically two choices for operating inset ailerons in foam wings. Firstly you will need a tube and cable which has been built into the foam before the veneers are applied which will exit the veneer at the appropriate scale point. The ailerons will be driven by a servo mounted in the centre of the wing. The alternative method is to use a pair of aileron servos which are directly connected to the aileron horn but provision for this will need to be made at the construction stage of the wing. A tube will need to have been cut in the foam cores enabling you to slide the wires for a servo down through the centre of the wing which is quite easy to do in the manufacturing stage but very difficult later on.

As you may have already realised, fitting inset ailerons to a foam wing is a little harder than to the equivalent built up wing. When you start to fit scale flaps and scale retracts these create even greater problems. With the retract unit you will need to reinforce quite a large area of the wing to spread the load – as already mentioned, foam will give little support to the hardwood bearers that are so essential to fix the retract units to. If you were using a traditional built-up wing you would only need to apply ¹⁄₁₆" ply doublers to the sides of the affected wing ribs to increase their strength considerably and make it a simple job to install the retract units.

If the retract units were fairly close to the centre of the wing then it would be beneficial to carry the bearers through to the centre to be covered with the glassfibre bandage as already suggested for the torsion bar undercarriage. If on the other hand they are further out from the centre there is little point in trying to do this.

Generally when you are working with white foam core wings it is worth remembering that most of the spirit based adhesives will dissolve the foam cores. If you are in any doubt check before you start using a particular type of adhesive.

As already mentioned, polyester or normal glassfibre resins will dissolve foam along with Evostick Impact and some paints will also attack foam. The white PVA glues

A much better method is to use a filler such as Polyfilla or microballoons mixed with polyester resin which can then be spread onto the veneer and blended in to the glassfibre bandage. It is now an easy job to lightly sand the filler down to blend in with the top of the glassfibre. It is also a good idea to give the glassfibre a light coat of filler so that you only need to rub the high spots down. See Fig.2 for details.

If your aircraft is a low wing design it may well have a torsion bar undercarriage. These are usually fitted to the model by using a ¼" ply by 1" wide strip which is let into the foam core wings and then the undercarriage leg is fastened with aluminium or plastic saddle clamps screwed in place. It is far better if this ply fixing plate is carried right through to the centre of the wing so that when the glassfibre bandage is applied to join the wings, the undercarriage fixing plate is also glassfibred in place.

It is worth remembering that anything you stick to the foam will need to be a very rigid fixing and additions such as the undercarriage are a high stress item and can pull out of a foam core wing if not very securing attached. See Fig.3 for details.

There are various ways of operating ailerons on foam core wing models. The simplest type of aileron which is used extensively on aerobatic models are called strip ailerons. Basically these are a full span aileron with only the last few inches against the fuselage side being fixed. These ailerons are invariably operated by torque rods which are attached to the trailing edge of the wing. Fig.4 gives details of this general arrangement.

Most fullsize aircraft feature some form of inset aileron. Provision for this will need to have been built in

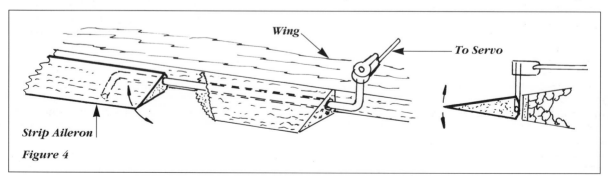

Labels in figure: Wing, To Servo, Strip Aileron

Figure 4

The author's HD-1 in its attractive five colour camouflage scheme. There are some 44 wing ribs on the top wing alone in this aircraft. If you had to cut them by hand it would be quite a lengthy job.

work perfectly well as does Copydex which can be used as an impact adhesive although it is not particularly strong. Epoxies do not seem to attack white polystyrene foam. Some high quality foam core wings use a blue foam which is better in respect of some of the adhesives that can be used with it but it is always best to check on a scrap piece first.

Built Up Wing Construction

As we have already had a look at foam wing construction it has become obvious that they have certain limitations for use within scale models. The alternative method of construction is a traditional built up wing with individual balsa or light ply ribs with balsa or spruce spars. With this method of construction you can build the thin undercambered wings of the early bi-planes such as those used in WW1. The thick, semi or fully symmetrical, all sheeted wing of the WW2 fighter or modern aerobatic aircraft can also be built using this method.

If the aircraft is to feature retracts, flaps or any other specialised equipment, providing it is thought out at the design stage it causes little in the way of problems or additional weight.

Twin engined models will need engine nacelles built into the wing and are a hundred times easier with a built up structure than they are with foam wings!

Assuming that you are either designing your own model or building from a plan, you will need to make a number of identical wing ribs for a parallel cord wing using a template or, if your aircraft has a tapered wing,

then the ribs will need to be cut using the sandwich method.

Cutting Wing Ribs

When building a constant cord wing you will need to cut a template from which all the balsa wing ribs can be cut and transferring the information from the drawing to the ply sometimes seems to give people a little bit of a problem.

There are various methods suggested for transferring the shape, such as using a pin to prick through the plan into the plywood underneath, removing the plan, joining up all the pin marks with a biro and then cutting through the line. Another method – but one which I haven't tried – is to get a section of the plan photocopied and then lay the copy onto the balsa wood or ply. Using a warm iron, iron the back of the paper and transfer the outline on to the material that way. One thing that needs to be borne in mind is that most photocopiers reduce the size of their copy from the original by a small amount. Some also appear to have a noticeable distortion on them as well, so that method does need to be used with some care.

The method I have found quite successful for transferring ribs or former shapes onto the balsa or plywood is to use a sheet of carbon paper on top of the ply or balsa and under the plan. If the carbon paper is first laid on the wood, preferably overhanging the material a little and carefully slid under the plan, it is quite easy to press down the plan and find the edge of the material underneath it. This process can be repeated a few times with

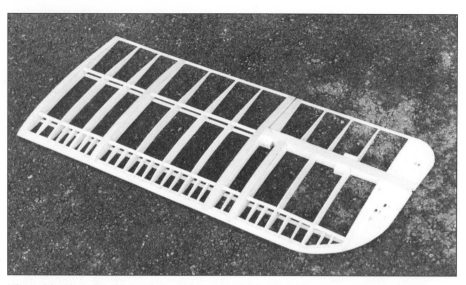

The author's SE5A top wing panel shows the typical construction for a WW1 bi-plane with the thin undercamber wings and many additional riblets.

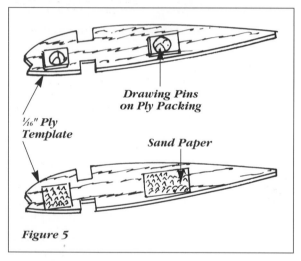

Figure 5

The author's 1/4 scale Sirocco with the basic wing ribs and spar structure built and having part of the top sheeting applied.

careful realigning and that way you can avoid quite a bit of waste of materials. When you are satisfied that they are in the right place get a fairly heavy object to place on the plan over the material. This will help hold the lot together and then an outline can be drawn around the rib, former or whatever using a ballpoint pen. Best is a biro that doesn't work thus avoiding marking the plan as all that is required is pressure to go through to the carbon paper to mark the plywood or balsa underneath.

Whilst marking the outline of the wing rib or former it is also worth adding centre lines which can be very useful at a later stage in the building to see whether the construction is lining up true. Any plywood of about ¹⁄₁₆" or ¹⁄₃₂" is quite suitable for use as a template for cutting wing ribs and if any of the wing ribs are going to require doublers then of course the doubler can actually be used as the template, thereby saving work at a later stage.

Now we have our piece of plywood with the outline of the wing rib marked on it we need to cut it to size and accurately shape it. Even ¹⁄₁₆" plywood can be cut to rough shape with a pair of scissors though it is a little bit like wood butchery! It can also be cut with a Stanley hand knife, though ¹⁄₁₆" ply is a little bit thick for the average modelling knife and certainly for a scalpel. The rib can be cut a little oversize then sanded to shape to produce a nice smooth edge which will make it easier to cut the subsequent balsa ribs.

Whilst one is preparing the template it is well worth cutting out notches for the wing spars or the leading edge, trailing edge or any additional spars that are going to go through all the wing ribs. At this stage it is not worth making any cutouts for undercarriage mounting as they will only be found on a few ribs.

Now the template is ready for use and can be laid straight onto the sheet of balsa and cut around with a scalpel. Some people seem to experience a problem with the template slipping around on the sheet of balsa underneath. There are two

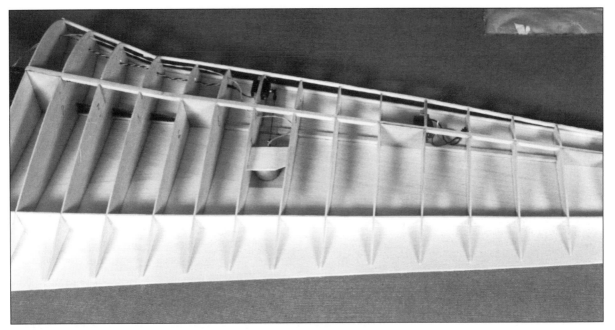

The tapered wing for the 1/6 scale Beech 18 being built by the author. Bottom sheeting has been applied with the servos also fixed in place before the top sheeting is attached.

quite simple methods of stopping this problem and a look at Fig.5 shows the ply rib template with a pair of drawing pins stuck through it, the points of which should be of sufficient length to just go into the balsa sheet. A little packing under the heads of the drawing pins – perhaps a piece of ⅛" sheet balsa or similar material – will help to give the correct length of pin sticking through on the underside. When the correct amount of packing has been found then the blocks and drawing pins can be stuck in place with 5 minute epoxy. An alternative method would be to cut a couple of squares of medium sandpaper and stick them to one side of the ply template as in Fig.5.

As most of the cutting of the wing rib will be across the grain it is always best if you cut in the direction which will produce a smooth edge in the cut. If you have ever cut across a piece of balsa wood at about say 45° to the grain you will notice that one edge of the cut is quite smooth and the other quite rough. If you look at Fig.6 you will note that the cuts are made from roughly the main spar position which is the thickest part of the wing rib towards the edges, cutting across the grain and producing a smooth edge on the wing rib. Whilst you are cutting out the wing rib, all the notches for spars, leading edge and perhaps some holes for the aileron pushrods can also be cut or drilled at the same time.

If the wing ribs you

have made are for a typical WW1 bi-plane then you will also need to cut a number of riblets. The same ply template can be used to cut the riblets but will obviously only need to be placed on the balsa to include the leading edge and spar cutouts.

Aircraft which have tapered wings will require the wing ribs to be made in a totally different way. If the plan you are working from shows the individual wing ribs then it is quite a practical proposition to use carbon paper to reproduce their shape directly onto balsa wood. When you have cut out one wing rib for each shape it will then be a simple enough job to cut out a second to produce the other wing panel. If of course you are designing your own model you will know what your wing root shape is against the fuselage and your wing tip section. On some plans this is all you will be shown so you will need to make the wing ribs by what is commonly known as the "sandwich" method.

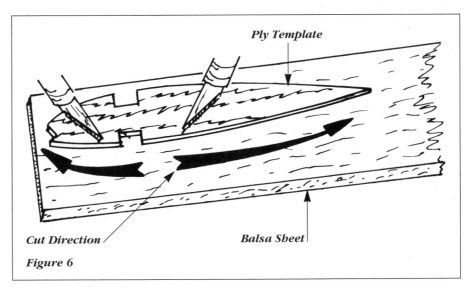

Ply Template

Cut Direction

Balsa Sheet

Figure 6

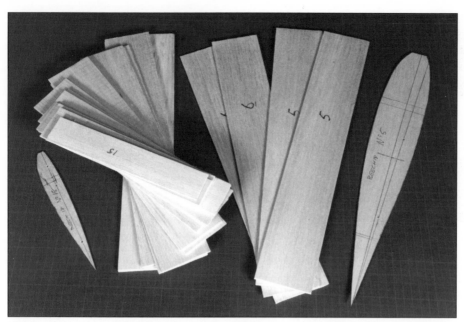

The two ply wing rib templates have been cut along with the blanks for making the wing ribs by the sandwich method.

Cutting Wing Ribs – Sandwich Method

This system can be extremely versatile and is certainly fairly easy to use on a wing that does not have a great deal of taper in it and preferably has a reasonable number of ribs as well. If this is the first time you intend to use the sandwich method then it would be best to avoid a highly tapered wing since this makes it far more tricky to produce the ribs accurately.

The main advantage of the sandwich method is that it can be used perfectly well for a wing which has a constant rate of taper and maintains the same wing section from root to tip or for an aircraft which has a changing wing section – for example, a semi-symmetrical section at the root and a slightly undercambered section at the tip. All this can be worked into the sandwich method with absolutely no trouble at all. At this stage do not cut out the wing spar cutouts as this is better done later, but laying the tip template on top of the root template and making sure that both the centre lines line up perfectly along with the marked position for the main spar.

When you are fully satisfied with the positioning, drill a pair of holes through the two templates on the centre line as far apart as you reasonably can to take the bolts which hold the entire sandwich of wood together. As these bolts often need to be several inches long but of quite small diameter it would be quite difficult to get hold of them commercially, so I have made my own using a pair of quick link rods. A couple of nuts on the threaded end gives you some adjustment. A pair of washers can be soldered roughly in the middle of the rods and these can be adjusted in position to suit the thickness of the pack of ribs that you are cutting. It is worth keeping them for future models that you may wish to build.

At this stage we are ready to start cutting the balsa blanks for making the ribs and as both the left and right hand wing ribs will be made simultaneously two blanks should be cut for each rib position (ie rib number 1 left and right and so on). The first few rib blanks will need to be cut larger than the biggest template then they can reduce in size towards the tip. If you don't quite get it right then you can finish with having some only partially formed wing ribs which have to be thrown away – that comment comes from experience! All the rib blanks will need drilling for the bolts which can now be fitted.

Bolt the entire pack together and it will now be fairly obvious why this method of making wing ribs is called the sandwich method. With the sandwich assembled and put in a bench vice to hold lightly, roughly shape it with either a sharp 1" chisel or razor plane then get to the

All the balsa blanks bolted together with the template ribs each side.

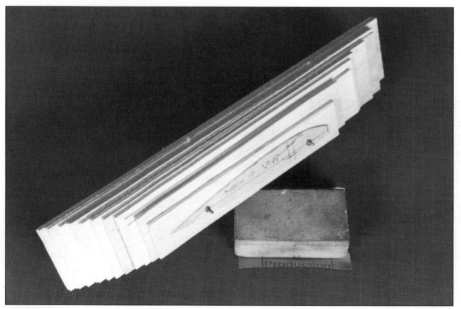

Scale Construction

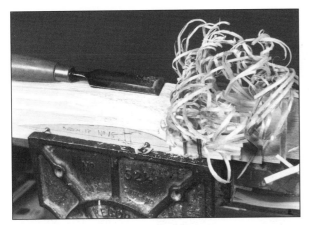

Carving the ribs to rough shape using a very sharp 1" chisel.

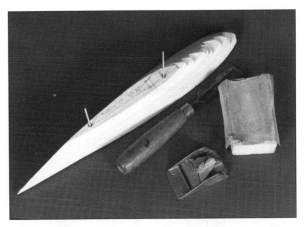

The complete sandwich of wing ribs have been sanded to their correct shape and are awaiting the leading edges to be trimmed as well. Also the spar cut-out position has been marked.

final shape using sandpaper on a large sandpaper block which will produce a much smoother result. When you are completely satisfied that you have a good shape on the top and bottom and everything is really smooth you can now consider making the cutouts for the main spars. This can quite easily be done using something like a junior hacksaw and making the vertical cuts with that. Numerous cuts can be made in the spar slots so that the entire cutout can almost be chipped out using a saw. By carefully working the saw in the groove from side to side the bottom of the groove can be kept quite clean. The cutout for the leading edge can be made at the same time along with any other cutouts or holes. Dismantle the entire pack of ribs but do it carefully so that all the ribs are retained in their correct sequence since each rib will be a slightly different size to its neighbour.

Mark the first pair of ribs number 1, the next pair number 2 etc. until the tip rib is reached. Take the first pair with the smaller of the two ribs on top and your sandpaper block with some medium sandpaper on it and sand the larger of the two ribs down to the same size as the smaller ones, thereby making sure they are both the same size. Make sure that you do not lose the position of one rib upon the other. At the same time you can, with a sharp scalpel, cut out the wing spar depth a little, equalling up the top rib – the leading edge cutout can be done at the same time in the same way. This

process will need to be carried out on all the pairs of wing ribs until you have a complete set of wing ribs for a tapered wing.

Although it sounds a rather laborious and time-consuming job, in fact it doesn't really need to be much more than an evening's work to produce the complete set of wing ribs for your model.

Wing Spars

We now have a pile of wing ribs ready to assemble onto the spars to start building the wing. A little consideration needs to be given to the selection of materials for wing spars as these are very much a structural item. Early aircraft with their thin, undercambered wing sections could not be built strong enough to sustain flight without folding or breaking with dire consequences. If they built a monoplane which was to have sufficient integral strength this could only effectively be achieved by using additional bracing wires attached to the undercarriage and a pillar mounted above the fuselage. With this additional bracing the aircraft could be made sufficiently strong to handle normal flight requirements.

The wings on the Antanov are removable from the side of the fuselage and the attachments can be seen along with the aileron and flap linkage. A removable hatch is used to gain access to this essential equipment.

The sandwich of ribs dismantled and with the spar cut-outs.

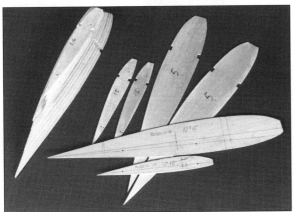

The Antanov fully rigged has very successfully concealed the method which is used to dismantle the model for transportation purposes.

The alternative and far more practical system used in the period was to go for the bi-plane configuration with interwing struts. These wingbays could be very easily braced and would give considerable strength to what was a fairly flimsy airframe. It was only in later years when engine performance improved considerably and aircraft design moved to the much thicker semi symmetrical wing that the spars could be built in far enough apart to produce a wing with sufficient integral strength. This had the great advantage of not requiring any bracing wires which impart a lot of drag to an aircraft.

On the typical WW2 fighters with the thicker wing sections the wing would also be completely metal covered – this was called monocoque construction. The entire package contributed to the strength of the wing rather than just relying on the internal, fabric covered structure of the WW1 bi-plane. Also with the thicker wings it was possible to fit vertical webbing to the spars which would then convert two individual spars to something that approximated an "I" section girder. This contributes tremendous strength without a great deal of weight. When you think about the loads put upon wing spars in flight under normal conditions the bottom spar would be under a tensile load which does not seem to be the problem. When a wing folds, invariably it seems to be caused by the top spar compressing and folding, allowing the wing to bend with predictable consequences!

The vertical webbing applied to the spars will considerably reduce the risk of the top spar pressing inwards and will also have the effect of stopping the two spars moving in relation to each as they will now be

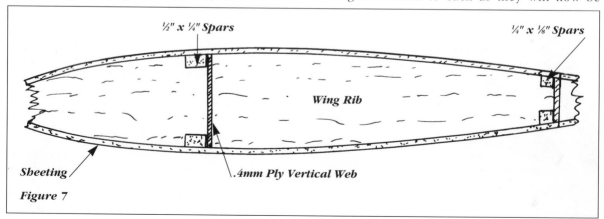

½" x ¼" Spars

¼" x ⅛" Spars

Wing Rib

Sheeting

.4mm Ply Vertical Web

Figure 7

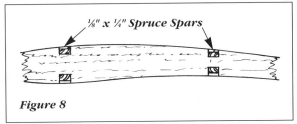

Figure 8

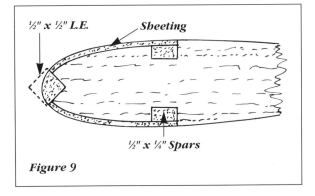

Figure 9

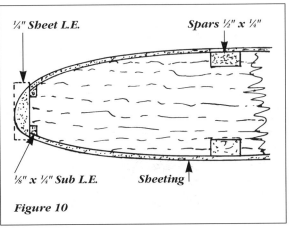

Figure 10

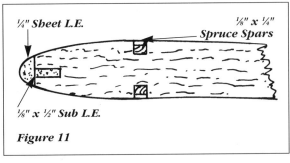

Figure 11

permanently bonded. On a model even ¹⁄₁₆" balsa will achieve a very effective vertical web but an even better material is .4mm ply as this is quite a rigid product whilst being very light and thin. Vertical webs can also be added to the spars of the early WW1 bi-planes and that will make the wing quite a bit more rigid. It is also worth trying to keep the spars as far apart as you can and as close to the surface as possible for the greatest strength.

If the wing is to be fabric covered then you will obviously need to keep the spars sufficiently below the surface to avoid the material sag between the ribs touching the tops of the spars which will ruin the appearance of the wings. On quarter scale aircraft such as my SE5A and DH Tiger Moth I have used ⅛" x ¼" spruce spars back and front within ³⁄₃₂" sheet hard balsa ribs. The models have functional rigging wires fitted to the wings which are sufficiently strong to withstand normal flight loads. With an all sheeted wing of perhaps 70" to 90" span, ½" x ¼" medium to hard balsa spars would be perfectly adequate especially if the wing was fully sheeted. If you are trying to save every half ounce and the wing is tapered you may wish to taper the spars from ½" x ¼" at the wing root to ¼" x ¼" at the tip – this would be easy to accommodate if you are making the wing ribs by the sandwich method previously described. If the all-sheeted wing has inset ailerons and flaps then rear spars may be useful to form the trailing edge of the wing where the flaps and ailerons are attached. These spars can be quite small and ⅛" x ¼" medium balsa would be more than adequate.

When the wing is complete and the ailerons and flaps cut away you may wish to apply ¹⁄₁₆" balsa sheet vertically to seal the trailing edge. Fig.7 illustrates a semi or fully symmetric wing section with balsa ribs and vertical webs whilst Fig.8 illustrates a typical thin undercamber wing for an early bi-plane.

Wing Leading Edge

Another part of the wing construction which is worth careful consideration is the leading edge. One of the more popular methods of building a leading edge is the "D" section. This basically consists of the front portion of the wing from the leading edge to the spars being sheeted with the rear portion mainly fabric covered. The leading edge on this type of wing could be described as a birds mouth where a V is cut into the leading edge of the rib and typically a ½" x ½" medium balsa let in. When the top and bottom sheeting is applied the leading edge can then be sanded to form the true section. Fig.9 illustrates the "D" box construction, but the actual leading edge method could be used on a fully sheeted wing with equal success. I have used this method on a number of models myself over the years.

The alternative method I have used on fully sheeted wings is to use a piece of quarter sheet balsa of the appropriate width stuck straight to the front of the ribs.

When you sheet the top and bottom of the wing you butt the covering up against the leading edge and then sand the quarter sheet to form the leading edge section. The slight problem with this I have found is that when you start to sand the top and bottom covering between the ribs it may go down on you slightly if it isn't stuck very securely to the leading edge. The improvement on this system which I am currently using on the 1/6th scale Beech 18 I am building, is to use a false leading edge made from two pieces of ⅛" x ¼" glued to the front of the rib. When the glue has dried the top and bottom of these pieces can be sanded to blend in with the rib section.

The top and bottom wing sheeting can now be applied and glued to these false leading edges. The quarter sheet leading edge can then be stuck in place and when it is sanded to the airfoil section the false inner leading edges will support the top and bottom sheeting allowing you to sand the whole area and blend it in perfectly. Fig.10 illustrates this system which is equally applicable to a fully sheeted wing or a D box section. Fig.11 shows the leading edges which I have

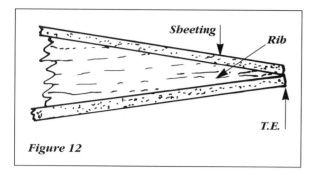

Figure 12

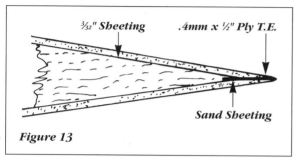

Figure 13

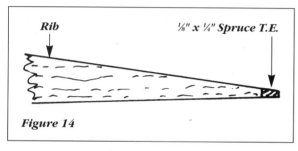

Figure 14

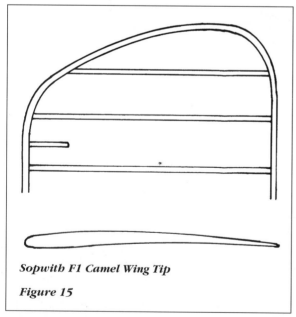

Sopwith F1 Camel Wing Tip

Figure 15

used successfully on my quarter scale DH Tiger Moth and Hanriot HD-1. The front of the rib has a slot cut to accept the ½" x ⅛" medium balsa sub leading edge. The leading edge proper is then made from quarter sheet and stuck onto the front of the ribs and the sub leading edge. Since this type of wing is fabric covered there will

be no strength given to the wing by any sheeting. In the event of the model being hit between the ribs on the leading edge, without the sub spar it would be very easy to damage the model so the combination of the leading edge and the sub leading edge will give quite a lot of strength to this area.

Wing Trailing Edge

The trailing edge of the wing is also something that is worth considering before you commence building the model. On sport models it is very common for the wings to be sheeted with $\frac{3}{32}$" balsa as it is on scale models. It is common to see this sheeting brought to the trailing edge where you then have two thicknesses of $\frac{3}{32}$" giving a $\frac{3}{16}$" trailing edge. If you multiply that figure by 4 or 6 (depending on the scale of your model) to equate it to a fullsize aircraft it will make you realise just how non scale that sort of trailing edge is.

If you look at a modern jet fighter, the trailing edge is almost razor sharp which is important for efficient aero-dynamics of a wing! Fig.12 gives a good example of how not to make a decent looking scale model. Fig.13 shows a far better way of doing it and the main secret here is to use a strip of .4mm ply which only needs to be about ½" wide although it could be up to 1" if you preferred. If you tried sanding the balsa down to a feather edge it would present no problems at all but it doesn't take much to realise that there would be no structural strength in the trailing edge and every time you moved the wing it would get damaged. Inserting the ply will contribute a great deal of strength to the trailing edge and will make it far less susceptible to 'hangar rash'.

With an undercambered wing such as that used on WW1 bi-planes I have used a ⅛" x ¼" spruce stuck directly to the rear of the wing rib. See Fig.14. It is best if it is stuck with a PVA white glue rather than trying to superglue it into place as cyano does not always work effectively on spruce. The trailing edge can then be sanded to blend in with the rib section whilst trying to keep the trailing edge looking reasonably thin. It is quite surprising how noticeable and out of place a thick trailing edge looks on an otherwise good scale model so it is well worth going to that little bit of extra trouble to try and keep it as thin as you can whilst maintaining reasonable strength.

Wing Tips

Wing tips can be a very distinctive part of any fullsize aircraft and there seems to be as many types as there are aircraft designs. On an all sheeted wing with a rounded tip it is simplest to carry the sheeting on from the last rib and bring the top and bottom sheeting together to form the desired shape. The alternative would be to carve the tips from solid or build them up using laminations of quarter sheet which would enable you to cut out lightening portions within the block to save weight. The wing tips on the early bi-planes in some cases can be built up using ⅛" sheet balsa to form the scale outline and the covering will flow from the last rib around the tip to produce the correct scale shape. As an alternative to this system you may wish to use the laminated method which I will now describe. This method can also be used very successfully for making fuselage formers if you particularly wish to save space or make a thin former that will be visible within the cockpit area.

Laminated Wing Tips

It is only really worth using a laminated tip where it is a particularly awkward curved shape and even then it is only really necessary where the model is going to have a translucent covering through which, when the model is flying on a bright sunny day, you can see the ribs and spars. Generally the aircraft that require this type of treatment are WW1 bi-planes or aircraft of that period. One which readily springs to mind would be the Curtiss Jenny that was very frequently just covered in the basic material and didn't receive any further painting. The Sopwith Camel is another such subject as the shape of the tip could very easily be made as a laminated tip – a look at Fig.15 will show the plan form of the tip.

It is also worth noting that with the undercamber section of the wings for that period (also see Fig.15), not only does the tip have to be curved in plan form but it also has to be shaped quite a bit in profile to maintain the undercamber section of the wing at the tip. A look at Fig.16 will show the general method of constructing a laminated wing tip.

The plywood block template is cut to the outside shape of the wing tip to be formed. The laminations can be in the form of two or preferably three thin layers of balsa. This could be 1/16" sheet or even a combination of sheets of 1/16" balsa and .4mm ply which also bends extremely well and would certainly produce a very strong and light tip. The laminations need to be put into the template one at a time and will almost certainly will need soaking in water first to get them to bend if the radius is at all tight. Once the wood is wet, the type of glue you use has to be a glue which is compatible with water so will have to be one of the white PVA glues which we would normally use for modelling in any case. If that gets a bit watered down it will make no difference to the finished strength of the job. Each layer will need glue in between and it is best to put one layer in at

a time gently holding them in place with pins whilst the next layer is put in.

If it is only a fairly small tip that you are doing then you do not even need to go to the trouble of cutting out a piece of plywood as in Fig.16. Instead the outside shape can just be a row of pins stuck into the plan to form the outside shape and the pieces of balsa pushed up against the pins with additional pins on the inside to hold it all in place. If you are doing a somewhat deeper tip then it is best to go to something like a piece of plywood or chipboard to form the template and you can use several blocks inside to hold the laminations in place. To prevent your laminations sticking firmly to your template it is a good idea to stick something like Sellotape or the wider sort of brown packing tape to the inside edge of the template to stop any glue sticking to that and of course when you place your template over the plan do lay a sheet of polythene over the plan to stop that sticking as well. When the laminations have been glued and you are satisfied that all your strips of wood are stuck firmly together, leave them to dry for at least 24 hours – preferably 48 hours. They can then be removed and trimmed down to length. It is always a good idea to leave the wood a little on the long side as it is easier to trim some surplus off later. When fixing a laminated tip to the trailing edge and leading edge of the wing it is better to join it by splicing it over an inch or two if you possibly can to give the greatest strength at the joint.

Aileron Design and Construction

When a choice of aircraft is made it is likely to be based on personal preference but the aircraft's flying characteristics may also have a strong influence on your decision. You would naturally expect an aircraft such as a WW1 bi-plane to be a fairly slow flying model with forgiving characteristics whilst a WW2 fighter would be a much faster flying aircraft but would be far more 'groovy' and suitable for flying in a wide choice of weather conditions.

Aircraft such as a WW1 bi-plane and WW2 fighter

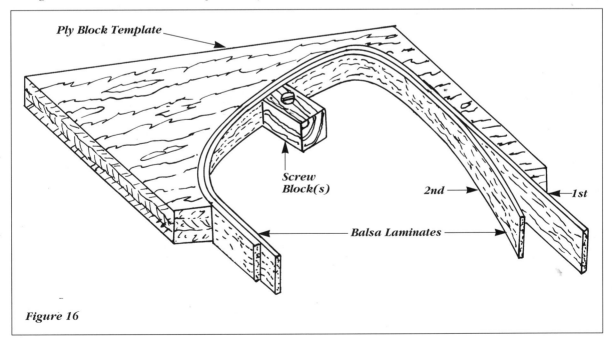

Ply Block Template

Screw Block(s)

2nd   1st

Balsa Laminates

Figure 16

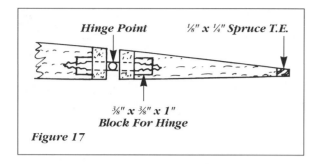

Hinge Point   ⅛" x ¼" **Spruce T.E.**

⅜" x ⅜" x 1"
Block For Hinge

Figure 17

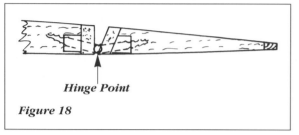

Hinge Point

Figure 18

obviously have different handling and flying characteristics yet why is it that two very similar aircraft can handle in such a different way? Obviously the size and positions of the control surfaces will have quite an influence on the handling but also the design of the control surfaces – particularly the ailerons – can have a very large effect on the aircraft.

When I design a scale model the external shape of the aircraft has already been designed for me. If you wish to reproduce the fullsize handling characteristics as closely as possible then it is a good idea to incorporate the control surface design characteristics of your subject as well. This will also be important to the final appearance of the aircraft. On the early aircraft such as WW1 bi-planes the ailerons were of a very simple nature, having a square leading edge to the aileron butting up against the rear spar, usually with a centre hinge. See Fig.17. I have seen aircraft of this period with top and bottom hinged ailerons but still of a very basic nature.

My Hanriot HD-1 has bottom hinged ailerons which work well on the top wing. See Fig.18. As these aircraft

Two SE5A's built at almost quarter scale. The one in the foreground is Ken Forty's review model whilst the other was built by the author. Both these aircraft feature thin trailing edges which would be so important for the scale appearance of an aircraft such as this.

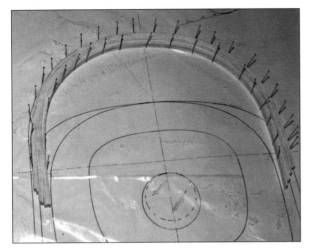

One of the fuselage formers for the Miles Gemini twin was fabricated using the laminated method. As there was no tight radius it was sufficient to use pins to form the shape.

The aileron gap on the fullsize Bristol Fighter has a slightly rounded leading edge to the aileron and a centre hinge. This aircraft is part of the Shuttleworth Collection.

used a closed loop system to operate the ailerons it meant that they were having almost equal up and down movement. It was taken for granted that when you flew one of these aircraft you would also apply quite a lot of rudder in the direction you wished to turn as well as applying ailerons. Some of these aircraft had the reputation that if you did not use rudder you would suffer what was known as adverse yaw from the ailerons. The effect of this is that if you apply right aileron alone you will find the aircraft turning to the left on you! This is caused mostly by the down going aileron on the outside of the turn producing more drag than the up going aileron on the inside of the turn.

Later aircraft such as the DH Tiger Moth used a different system for driving the ailerons on the lower wing which enabled them to incorporate a large amount of differential movement. This basically meant that when you applied right aileron the right aileron moved up whilst the left aileron hardly moved at all. This got over the problem of the down going aileron producing more drag and improved the problem of adverse yaw quite considerably although, I gather that when flying a fullsize Tiger Moth the rudder is still a very important control and needs to be nicely harmonised with the ailerons to fly the aircraft smoothly.

On my SE5A and Hanriot HD-1 I have individual aileron servos for each aileron and have incorporated quite a large amount of differential aileron which has improved the handling characteristics considerably without having an adverse effect on the scale appearance of the

aircraft. I can fly the SE5A, Hanriot and Tiger Moth quite comfortably using ailerons and elevator although for crisper control it is still useful to use the rudder at times.

Even some modern light aircraft such as the Sirocco which I have modelled use this type of aileron with a closed loop system so of course you get equal up and down movement. However, as the wing is quite a short stubby affair it does not seem to have an adverse effect on the flying qualities of this aircraft. See Fig.19. Another interesting feature of this aircraft is that the gap between the ailerons is sealed on the fullsize aircraft with a soft piece of fabric on the top of the aileron, see Fig.19. I have reproduced this effect on my model using a piece of Solarfilm ironed on after the model has been painted which works well.

The effects of adverse yaw do not seem to be too much of a problem on the lower aspect ratio wings but can be on the longer wings of gliders some WW2 type fighters.

To get over adverse yaw, the frieze type aileron

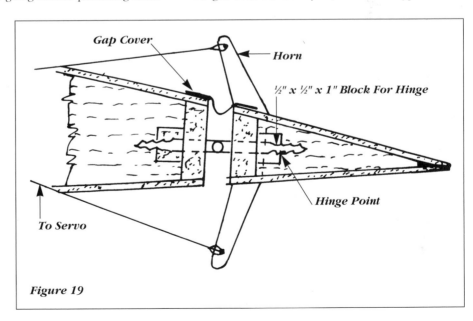

Gap Cover

Horn

½" x ½" x 1" Block For Hinge

Hinge Point

To Servo

Figure 19

The author's Miles Gemini twin with the right aileron up clearly illustrates the way the frieze aileron works.

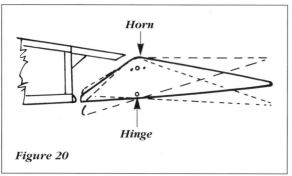

Figure 20

Differential movement will also be incorporated into the design so the left hand aileron will not go down very far and will not produce very much drag on the outside of the turn where it is not wanted. This type of aileron design only seems to appear on the semi symmetrical wing sections of the aircraft of WW2 or later. An aileron design such as this might well not be suited to an out-and-out aerobatic aircraft as it may start to initiate a turn when you would prefer to have a straight roll.

Looking at Fig.20, you will notice that the hinge point is very close to the bottom of the aileron whilst the pushrod is connected directly above it close to the top of the aileron. When designing a model, the further you can keep the horn/pushrod and hinge point apart the better it will be as the mechanical effects and slop will be working more in your favour. Fig.21 gives you an idea of how a frieze aileron would be constructed with the leading edge of the aileron being made from quarter sheet or similar which will enable you to round the top edge of the aileron easily.

The rear edge of the wing can be faced with ⅛" sheet and ³⁄₃₂" sheet or similar used to fill in over the top of the gap. Notice that the grain will travel in the opposite direction to the wing sheeting to give it some strength. A triangular fillet mounted under this sheeting will help to support it quite considerably.

Fig.22 shows a similar aileron but in this instance the hinge is mounted at the top whilst the horn is mounted on the bottom of the aileron. A pushrod going directly to an aileron servo mounted this way can give you quite a positive set up and should be slop free. Fig.20 is very typical of the construction and shows the hinge point for the aileron on the inboard end of it whilst, if you look at the photo, you will notice that the outboard hinge is mounted below the surface of the wing. This photo also shows that even with a small amount of right up aileron the leading edge of the aileron is protruding below the bottom surface of the wing, producing drag and also some air should escape up through the gap between the aileron and the wing increasing the airflow speed over the top of the aileron and further assisting with the turning effect on the aircraft.

Frieze ailerons take a little more time and effort to construct and set up accurately than the simpler types of aileron. They give a far more scale appearance to the aircraft and will certainly produce superior flying qualities. See Fig.23.

seems to have come into its own and cured just about all the problems in one fell swoop. I have made a Miles Gemini twin which has frieze ailerons fitted to it and Fig.20 gives a general idea of the design principles. Because the hinge point is mounted some way behind the leading edge of the aileron, as the aileron trailing edge goes up, the leading edge moves down into the higher pressure air which is below the wing. If you imagine that you are doing a right hand turn, the right aileron will go up but the leading edge of this right aileron will move down into the higher pressure air creating drag. As, in this case, the right aileron is on the inside of the turn, creating drag will help to turn the aircraft which is extremely beneficial.

On some scale models it is very easy to use the Robart hinge points as there is a quarter inch gap between the trailing edge of, for example, the tailplane and the leading edge of the elevator. On the other hand some ailerons, particularly of the frieze variety, require the pivot point to be built into the aileron itself. The problem here is that there is quite a length of unsupported hinge point protruding from the trailing

To Servo

Fill In

Note Grain Direction

Horn

Hinge Bracket

Hinge

Figure 21

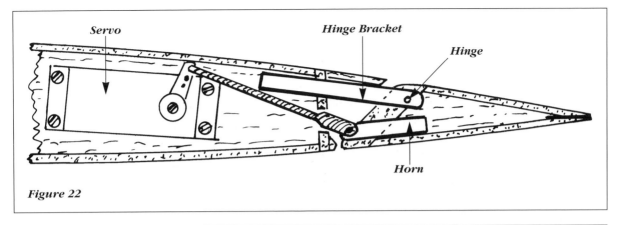

Figure 22

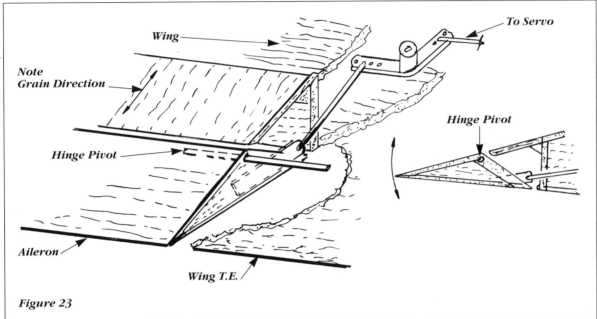

Figure 23

edge of the wing. This can obviously lead to a certain amount of flexing in the hinge which is obviously not desirable at all. A way of getting over this problem is to find some brass tube which will fit over the hinge point. The idea is to epoxy the hinge into the brass tube then epoxy the brass tube into the trailing edge of the wing. This should give good support to the actual pivot point of the hinge and generally increase the strength and rigidity of the hinge considerably. See Fig.24.

Dihedral Braces

On any one piece wing, some form of dihedral brace will be required. If you are building a bi-plane which is to have functional rigging wires and the wings are plugged onto each side of the fuselage with a top fixed-centre-section wing then maybe dihedral braces will not be required. Even if you are building a bi-plane which is to have one piece top and bottom wings you will still need to fit a dihedral brace, especially if you are not using any functional rigging wires.

In a small radio controlled scale model of perhaps 48" to 72" wing span, a piece of ⅛" ply would be adequate assuming the model was not particularly heavy. Aircraft above that sort of size would require at least ¼" thick ply.

Many years ago I suffered the indignity of having the

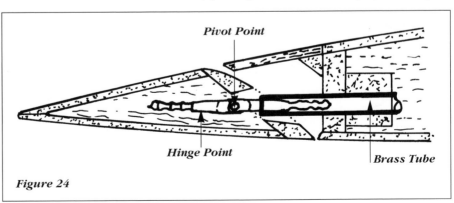

Figure 24

back of even a large estate car can prove quite difficult. The obvious solution to this is to build the wing in two parts and then slide them onto the fuselage with a detachable dihedral brace. I have seen this done using large diameter aluminium tube built into the fuselage with slightly larger diameter ones built into the wings. The two aluminium tubes will need to be tight fitting if you are to avoid any slop in the system. I have never personally used this system so have no experience of it but I understand these tubes are commercially available.

I am working on a 1/6th scale Beech 18 twin with a span of 96"

The frieze ailerons fitted to the Hawker Hind of the Shuttleworth aircraft Collection. With the aileron raised the leading edge protrudes below the bottom wing surface to create drag on the inside of the turn.

wings on a scale model fold in flight. There were quite a number of technical reasons why this happened but one of the things I noticed from the wreckage was that the ¼" ply dihedral brace, although remaining in one side of the wing, had come unglued from the wing spars in the other side. After giving this matter some considerable thought in subsequent models I have used four layers of ¹⁄₁₆" ply for the dihedral brace as opposed to ¼" ply. See Fig.25. Obviously this uses the same amount of wood and weighs much the same but will certainly be of superior strength. The great advantage I saw in this system was that you would have a far greater gluing area for the dihedral braces to the back and front spars which had been one of the causes of the failure of the model in flight. If you are designing your own model or working from a commercial plan it would be well worth considering whether to incorporate a feature such as this into your model.

With a number of scale models these days getting very large, transporting a 100" wing or similar in the

so I have opted for the two part wing. Instead of using the aluminium tube system I have made up carbon kevlar with epoxy dihedral braces which interlock on each other. There are two layers of carbon kevlar with an additional three tows of carbon let in against the top and bottom spars. The photo will give you a general idea of this arrangement.

Wing Building Sequence

So far we have had a look at the various methods of constructing a wing but a quick run through of the building sequence would also be beneficial. First of all it is very useful if you have a large flat building board that will enable you to build at least a complete wing panel in one go on it. Spread the plans out over the bench and cover with a sheet of polythene or backing from iron-on fabric coverings. This has the advantage of stopping your wing sticking to the plan and ruining it when you lift the wing off!

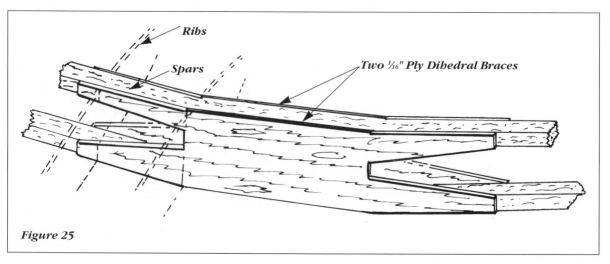

Ribs

Spars

Two ¹⁄₁₆" Ply Dihedral Braces

Figure 25

If you are building a semi symmetrical or fully symmetrical wing then the wing spars can be pinned directly to the building board. If on the other hand it is an undercambered wing section which, when completed, will be fabric covered the spars will need to be kept below the surface of the wing. For this you will need to put packing pieces of balsa onto the plan to raise the spars a sufficient height to allow the wing ribs to drop into their correct position.

If you are using aileron servos which are to be mounted into the wing ribs then you will need to stick some ¹⁄₁₆" ply to the side of the rib to fit the servos to. The details of this will be discussed later. You will also need to drill any holes required to take

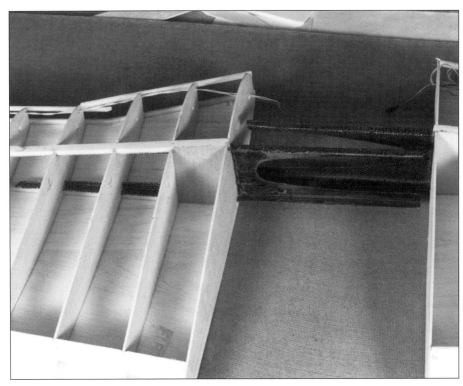

The carbon fibre dihedral braces will lock into each other when they are fastened in the fuselage. Note that the carbon fibre is carried through the wing beyond rib no.4. This is to spread the load on a much greater area of wing spar.

aileron servo or flap servo leads which can be done easily at this stage. You must also decide whether any holes are required for retract servo leads or tubes for pneumatic undercarriage retracts.

It is worth drilling a small hole in each wing rib so that, if the wing is to have an iron-on fabric covering, any air trapped between the ribs can escape otherwise the heat from the iron will cause the trapped air to expand and raise the covering causing difficulties at this stage.

When the wing ribs are ready they may now be glued in place and my personal preference is to use one of the PVA glues, although a lot of modellers nowadays prefer to use one of the cyanos.

With all the ribs stuck in place onto the bottom spars the top ones can be let in. Before the glue has had a chance to set make sure that all the wing ribs are vertical. The first rib which butts up against the side of the fuselage may need to be

set at an appropriate angle to adjust for the dihedral of the wing.

You can now build up the leading edge, the parts which can be completed at this stage before the wing sheeting is applied. Also if there is a separate trailing edge to be fitted that can be stuck in place now.

The outboard bracket for the aileron hinge is clearly visible in this photo. Note it is mounted below the aileron surface and also a distance from the leading edge of the aileron.

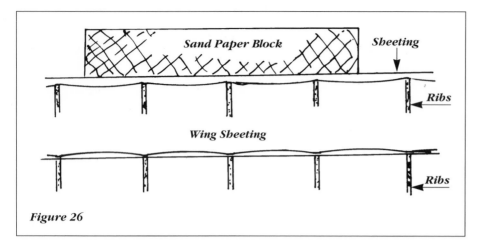

Figure 26

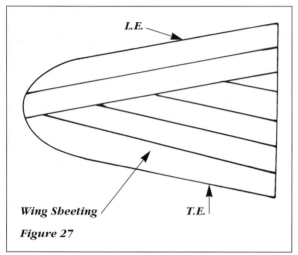

Wing Sheeting

Figure 27

from the sanding block and the areas you sand will be on top of the ribs because they are fully supported. This can result in the model taking on a "starved horse" appearance which will do nothing for the look of the aircraft. See Fig.26. The skins should be cut, fitted and glued together and allowed to thoroughly dry. See Fig.27. The back of the wing panel should be given a rough sanding to remove any high spots or lumps of glue whilst the face side will need a very good sanding. As this will be done on a flat surface it is very easy to do and achieve good flat results. Apply the bottom wing skin first. This may be done by applying beads of PVA glue to the tops of the ribs, spars, leading edge, trailing edge etc. and then pinning the sheeting on in one go.

Alternatively you may prefer to pin the sheeting in place without any glue. The advantage of this is that you can take your time pinning the sheeting in place and when you are completely satisfied with the fit you can use Superphatic which, with its thin tube dispenser, you can place in small beads on each side of the joint. This adhesive is designed to soak into the joint in much the same way as cyano does but without any of the problems or fumes which can upset you or stick your fingers permanently to everything in sight! Superphatic is fairly quick drying but it would be a good idea to leave it to thoroughly dry overnight before removing the pins.

When you have prepared the skin for the top of the wing as previously described put the wing back into the packing strips to make sure that you have the correct incidences on the root and tip as applying the second wing skin will determine the final shape that the wing adopts. The second wing skin you will have to stick on using beads of PVA glue on top of the ribs, spars, trailing edge etc. If you are to work .4mm ply into the trailing edge you will need to sand down the trailing edges of the top and bottom balsa sheets to accept this before the second sheet is applied.

If the model features inset ailerons on a fully sheeted wing these are built into the wing as an integral unit and then cut out at a later stage. You will need to then apply a facing piece to the aileron which is typically cut from quarter sheet.

Several of the diagrams on aileron construction will illustrate this point quite clearly. It is also worth noting that the fill-in piece above the aileron gap will need to have the grain direction running in the opposite direction to that of the spars. Depending on the type of dihedral brace or braces that your model has they may need building in before the second sheeting is applied although in some cases they may be fitted later. If you are building a bi-plane wing which is to be plugged onto the side of the fuselage, brass tubes will need to be let-in between the spruce wing spars and epoxied into position.

If the wing you are building is a tapered wing and all sheeted, you will need to have put a packing piece under the trailing edge of the wing to make sure that the wing ribs are at their correct incidences. There may also be washout built into the wing to improve the flight characteristics of the aircraft. This will also be described in far greater detail later.

The internal structure of the wing tips may now be added. Any additional reinforcing that is going to be required for undercarriage mounting blocks or any other pieces of equipment that will be built into the wing should also be done at this stage. If there are any vertical webs to be added now is the time they should be fitted.

If the wings are of all sheet construction you will need to lift the wing structure you have built off the building board and turn it upside down. With a very large sandpaper block and some fine to medium sandpaper it is a good idea to very lightly sand the bottom of the wing to make sure that all the ribs line up with each other and the spars do not protrude below the ribs. This only needs to be a very light sanding to remove any high spots and nothing more than that or you will change the wing section. It is far better to make up a complete wing skin on a flat building board rather than stick the individual sheets directly onto the ribs as however carefully you butt joint the sheets on a wing you will need to give the wing a good hard sanding. The problem here is that the balsa will spring away

Chapter 3

Wing Washout

The expression wing washout seems to get bandied around at the flying site quite regularly. It seems to be a term that not everybody fully understands or realises how beneficial it can be to your model aircraft. Even greater confusion seems to exist about how you actually build it into the model to make sure that you have the correct incidence on the root wing rib as well as the tip rib.

First of all we will start by looking at the part of the aircraft's flight pattern where wing washout may make life easier for the pilot. Let's assume that your aircraft is flying along in a straight and level attitude at normal cruising speeds, see Fig.28A. At this state the wings will have an angle of attack of perhaps one, two or three degrees depending on the speeds, wing loading and numerous other factors that we will not get involved with here. We know that if we slow the aircraft down but still wish to maintain straight and level flight we will need to raise the nose to increase the angle of attack of the wings so that they can generate more lift at lower speed to maintain straight and level flight. See Fig.28B Obviously there comes a point at which we can no longer maintain straight and level flight without the aircraft stopping flying. When we reach this stage it is referred to as "stalling" and is usually expected to take place when the aircraft is at an angle of around 12° to its flight path. I have used the figure 12° as this is a commonly quoted figure although it may vary from aircraft to aircraft depending on numerous factors involved on that specific aeroplane – aircraft that have a delta configuration will usually reach a higher angle of attack before they will stall.

Assuming that the aircraft we are flying has a constant chord wing – be it of a monoplane or bi-plane configu-ration – it will carry out what is known as a straight stall – in other words the nose will drop with the whole wing stalling. It might have a tendency for one wing tip or the other to drop first but this should not be too marked. If our aircraft has a tapered wing – almost certainly of the monoplane types – then you can expect one of the wing tips to stall before the middle of the wing. It doesn't take much to work out that at this point we have two situations on our hands; one the aircraft has stalled – in itself a problem – but if the wing tip stalled before the centre of the wing we will almost certainly have the aircraft on its side by now, a far more tricky situation to rectify, especially if you are on landing approach and at low altitude.

The characteristics I have just described with a tapered wing stall would be ideal for the entry of an aerobatic model into a spin but we would prefer to do that when we wish to rather than by accident! So how do we make a tapered wing as easy to fly as a constant chord version. Generally tapered wing aircraft are more attractive than their constant chord counterparts and regarded as more efficient as well so it would certainly be nice if they could be designed to be as inherently stable as the constant chord type. Enter this word called "washout" which seems to be the fix-it for all situations. It will not sort out every aircraft with a highly tapered wing but it will go a long way to curing most of them and make them perform an awful lot better in the stall situation than a non washed out wing.

What is washout I hear you ask? Very simply, the wing has been twisted. That is the end effect but I will explain more. Where the wing is against the fuselage (ie the wing root) the leading edge will be higher than the

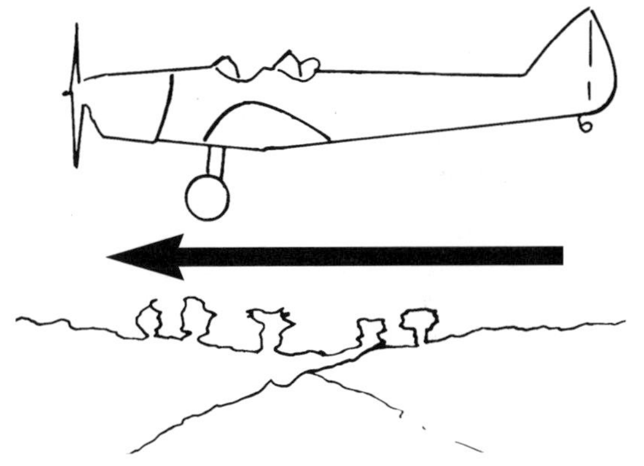

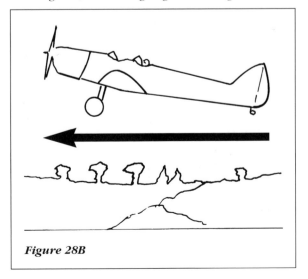

Figure 28A

Figure 28B

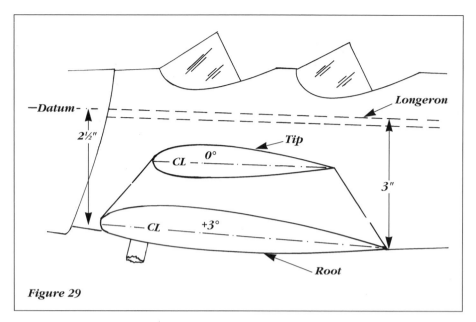

Figure 29

could well be at 0° meaning that the centre line of the tip rib is parallel with the datum line of the aircraft. It is now simple to work out that the wing has an overall twist of 3° in it. Now, if the aircraft is flying straight and level and the nose is very high we will assume that the fuselage datum line has reached an angle of attack of say 10°. In this situation the wing root (having 3° positive incidence) will be at 13° angle of attack. Meanwhile the wing tips (being at zero degrees to the datum line of the aircraft) will be at 10° to

trailing edge. If you have ever looked at the side view of a fuselage and the drawing of an aircraft there will almost certainly be a datum line drawn on it which in most cases will be parallel to the top fuselage longeron. All wing incidences are quoted from this datum line. If for instance the wing root is quoted as being +3° positive this will be in relation to the datum line and will mean that the leading edge is higher than the trailing edge by 3°. See Fig.29. If we now go to the wing tip this

the airflow. If we now think about those figures and bear in mind that the wing will stall at 12° the middle of the wing has probably just stalled whilst the wing tips are still flying and not stalled. The idea is that the middle of the wing will stall with both tips still flying which should produce a straight stall ie the nose of the aircraft goes down. As the wing tips never actually stalled there shouldn't be any tendency for the aircraft to want to drop a wing and put you into a spin which, on landing

The De Havilland Comet Racer has a highly tapered wing and would need more than just washout to make this a forgiving aircraft to fly. Even in experienced modellers hands this would be a very challenging aircraft.

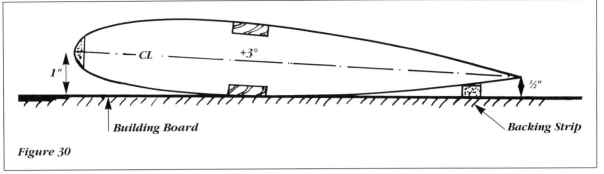

Figure 30

approach, would almost certainly spell disaster. I have quoted 3° of washout as it is a convenient figure to talk about and could well be used on a wing which has a severe taper such as the De Havilland 88 Comet twin-engined racing aircraft, although I do feel that a little more than wing washout would be required to make that particular aircraft a reliable and predictable scale model! Usually about 1° is quite adequate for a wing with less than 50° of taper on it. What does need to be remembered is that if the aircraft is inverted (eg at the top of a loop) this washout proceeds to work against you and can cause the aircraft to flick off the top of a loop. At least you have some altitude in your favour there!

Building In Wing Washout

When I make a built-up wing, especially if it is going to have washout built into it, I always draw the centre line on the root and tip rib. I start by pinning the main spar over the plan on the building board as my start point. By measuring the position of the root rib against the datum line of the aircraft I can determine how much

the leading edge is raised above the trailing edge which will indicate to me the position that it will need to be over the building board. If for example the leading edge of the root rib is 2½" from the fuselage datum line whilst the trailing edge is 3" to the datum line we need to have ½" difference on our wing rib. See Fig.30.

What I usually do is to use something like a piece of ½" balsa placed at the appropriate point under the rear of the wing rib. To find the correct position for this ½" square packing piece, simply move it backwards and forwards until you produce a ½" difference in the height of your centre line above the building board. Make sure that it is the leading edge which is ½" above the trailing edge. See Fig.30. The process can now be repeated on the tip rib, assuming that is at zero degrees which is of course parallel to the fuselage datum line and therefore parallel with the building board. Position the ½" square packing piece at the suitable point to make sure that the centre line is level or parallel with the building board. Pin the packing piece to the building board and note its position so that the wing on the other side can have its packing piece in exactly the same position. Complete building all the wing ribs, spars etc. and any other

The Westland Lysander has always been a popular aircraft to scale modellers as it exudes a wealth of character.

The author's Westland Lysander was built for the old light scale competition class and features the wing which incorporates quite a bit of washout within it.

internal structures into the wing. Remove the wing from this jig and apply the bottom wing sheeting. Allow the glue to dry, remove the pins etc. and put the wing back into the wing jig in exactly the place it was originally built ie the main spar over the plan in its correct position. This will re-jig the wing to its correct washout position and when you apply the top wing sheeting this will be in the correct place and the wing will be true.

One other question I get asked is whether it should be only the last two or three ribs that the washout is applied to or should the whole wing be twisted? On a scale model where appearance is important I always give the entire wing a gentle twist as this will make sure that you can maintain a straight leading and trailing edge. If it was only the last few ribs, there would be a pronounced kink in the trailing edge.

As a matter of interest, one of the other advantages of using wing washout on a scale model is because most fullsize aircraft have their wings mounted at least 3° or 4° positive. If we were to build a model with 3 to 4° positive on the wings, every time it flew fast it would want to go into a loop and every time we slowed down

it would want to go into a dive (you can imagine what fun that would be!).

It has been common practice on purpose-designed aerobatic models to rig them at zero right the way through which gets over any of the problems of the aircraft climbing and diving as we change speed. It would be simple enough to reduce the angle of attack on a scale model but this could upset the appearance of the aircraft where the wing joins the fuselage.

The way around this is to reduce the angle of attack by around 1° which would not be too noticeable but then wash the wing out to get rid of a lot of the angle of attack over the rest of the wing. This, coupled with a fairly forward centre of gravity, will produce an aircraft which should not 'balloon' on every speed change.

This is something I have found to be very useful and successful over recent years and has been incorporated into a number of the designs I have made.

Westland Lysander Wing

The Westland Lysander was a model I built a long time ago. If you are at all familiar with the aircraft you will know that it had quite a complicated wing and as the model was intended for the old light scale class the complete aircraft could not exceed 3kgs. My model had a span of 70" which worked out at a scale of 1.4:1. I also intended to have working flaps in addition to the leading edge slats!

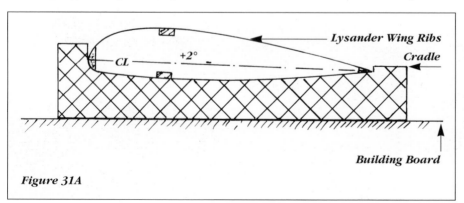

Figure 31A

As the Lysander is quite a complicated structure to build, it will be an interesting follow-on from the wing washout section and sandwich method previously described.

The wing starts very narrow at the fuselage root and widens at approximately one-third chord to its widest point before tapering again towards the wing tip. I designed the wing to have 2° positive angle of attack at the wing root and also at the widest point. The wing then tapers towards the tip which was set at 0°, giving the outer panel 2° of washout. This amount of washout, combined with a fairly forward centre of gravity gave the aircraft good, safe, low speed handling characteristics and the aircraft did not balloon at every change of speed the aircraft was asked to perform.

The wing ribs were made in two separate sandwiches as the widest rib was used as a template for both the inboard and outboard section of the wing. When it came to building the wing it was no use trying to pack up the trailing edge as previously described as there were two totally different portions to the wing.

The method I finally hit upon after much deliberation when designing the wing was to make three cradles out of quarter sheet balsa. Fig.31A is typical of the three cradles made for this wing. The individual cradles have the advantage of setting the wing at its correct incidence and also raising it the correct height from the building board to produce the dihedral. To make life even more interesting, neither the top or the bottom of the wing are built in a straight line since it tapers towards the tip and the root from the thickest point on the top and bottom. By raising the wing tips up in the cradle I was able to fix the brass tubes into the wing root which I used to align the separate wing panels onto the side of the canopy internal frame. Once the cradle had been built and set up I found the wing extremely easy to build and far quicker than I had expected. In fact in about four days I had the basic wing structure complete which turned out to be somewhat easier to build than it is to try to write and describe the process!

Rigging A Bi-Plane

The question of "How long does it take to rig a bi-plane on a cold day with frozen fingers" has been the subject of much jesting over the years! When looking at the subject of designing a bi-plane, it would seem quite logical – in modeller's eyes at least – to build the top and bottom wings as one-piece items We do that most of the time with monoplanes and that works perfectly well.

Going back a few years to when models were generally smaller than they are now, it was quite logical to use a one-piece top and bottom wing as they could be designed with sufficient strength to not require functional bracing wires which made life a lot easier. With the general increase of size in model aircraft, functional rigging wires have become almost a necessity on the larger and heavier models. Also if one is using a scale wing section on a typical WW1 type bi-plane, even using spruce spars and webbing, it would still be difficult – if not impossible – to make a wing which was sufficiently strong to be flown without rigging wires on anything but the smallest and lightest of scale models.

This photo clearly shows the double taper of the Westland Lysander wing, the outer section of which has at least 2° of washout built into it.

The Tiger Moth fuselage has 10swg rods protruding from it and the scale fuel tank along with the socket for the aileron servo. The top wing has the brass tubes let-in between the spars which makes for easy assembly of the aircraft at the flying field. Note also the aileron extension lead plug protruding from the lower wing tip as well as the ply retainer blocks with their "T" nuts and bolts in place.

If the wings on a WW1 bi-plane cannot be built strong enough without relying on functional rigging wires (and it would seem quite logical that they couldn't since the fullsize aircraft were much dependant on rigging wires for their integral strength) why should a modeller want to do it any differently.

The only problem that aeromodellers have that full-size aviators don't is that they wish to dismantle their aircraft at the end of a flying season pack it into the back of the car to drive it home! If the top and bottom wings are built in one piece the top wing can be removed from the cabane centre sections by various means but you will also need to remove the interwing struts and detach the rigging wires from one end in order to fold them against the wing surface at the other. The bottom wings could then be unbolted from the fuselage much as one does on a monoplane. Quite a few of the early bi-planes had the bottom wing mounted on the side of the fuselage over the undercarriage which might present some problems in detaching it from the fuselage.

A feature which is very useful for the modeller is the fact that a lot of bi-planes have their main wing panels made as separate items to the centre section and are bolted onto the main part of the wings. Three bi-planes which I have modelled over the last few years are the SE5A, De Havilland Tiger Moth and Hanriot HD-1 all at quarter scale.

The main wing panels on the SE5A have a pronounced gap between the centre section wing which is fixed to either the fuselage or the top of the cabane struts.

The Tiger Moth top wing fastens against the side of the scale fuel tank whilst the bottom wing touches the side of the lower fuselage and the trailing edge is actually below the fuselage line with a gap between it in plan form as well.

With the Hanriot HD-1 the bottom wings fasten against the side of the fuselage and the top wings meet in the middle because there is no separate centre section as on the SE5A. The fact that these three bi-planes all use the same basic system clearly illustrates how versatile this method of rigging can be.

Thinking about these aircraft at the design stage, it seemed far more practical to use 10swg wire which would protrude from the centre section wings and let brass tube into the outer wing panels between the spruce spars which would enable the wings to slide onto the centre sections. Having done that, it would enable me to leave the interwing struts permanently in place between the top and bottom wing panels on each side and all the bracing wires attached to the wings could also be left as integral units. All I now had to detach were the rigging wires where they met the side of the fuselage and the lower wing point. At this point a 6BA bolt has been let into the fuselage and, with a suitable bracket attached to the end rigging wires, this can be let over the 6BA bolt with a lock nut applied to the bolt to keep it in place. All that is now needed is a small strip of metal applied to the underside of the wings which can have a self-tapping screw put through the end of it which will lock it to the centre section wings. The purpose of this strip is purely to stop the wing sliding off the 10swg rods which will obviously be a disaster if it happened in flight!

You are probably wandering how I connected the aileron linkage and what effect it would have if the wings moved at all in flight. With the larger models it seems far simpler to use individual aileron servos mounted within the bottom wing driving the top wing aileron through a push-pull wire system which seems to work very well for the SE5A. To connect the aileron servo I mounted a socket in the lower wing stub and have an extended aileron servo lead protruding through the wing rib which is plugged into the socket

The Tiger Moth wings with the ply transportation plates in place. Note that the 4BA bolts fit nicely in the brass tubes which are built into the wing spars of the wing.

prior to fully assembling the aircraft. Building the SE5A and rigging it this way consists now of nothing more than plugging in two aileron servos, sliding the top and bottom wings on each side, screwing in six self-tapping screws, fixing four 6BA lock nuts in place and the aircraft is ready for flight. To date this aircraft has has 120 flights and over 21 hours flying time and has been rigged and dismantled more times than I care to remember.

The Tiger Moth, which was designed after the SE5A, applied the same basic principles again using two 10swg wire rods protruding from the scale fuel tank and one from the lower portion of the fuselage. These slide into brass tubes in the wing spars. The rear attachment to the lower wing on the bottom spar is a totally different fixing since, as previously mentioned, the wing at this point is well clear of the fuselage. Here I have a half inch wide steel strip of metal which goes right across the fuselage and protrudes through each side with a hole drilled through it to clear a 6BA bolt. On the wings I have a fixing bracket which has the 6BA bolt mounted in it and which has been screwed to the top of the spruce spars. When this is mounted on the wing and fixed to the fuselage I use a 6BA nylon lock nut to hold it in place. To

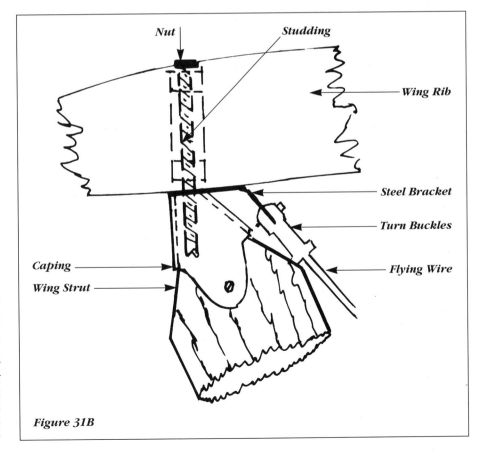

Figure 31B

stop the top and bottom wings sliding off the 10swg rods I have left a piece of ⅛" ply a 1" wide straight through the glassfibre scale fuel tank so that it protrudes roughly an inch each side and has an M4 T-nut let into it. This locates in a hardwood block mounted to the insides of the last wing rib and when the wing has been slid into position an M4 bolt goes through the hardwood block and secures to the T-nut stopping the wing sliding off. On the bottom wing, just behind the front spars, I have a similar piece of ply going across the fuselage which is fixed in he same way. All that I need to do to rig this aircraft is plug in the aileron servo, slide on the wing panels, secure them with four M4 bolts and two nylon lock nuts and the aircraft is ready to fly.

With the Hanriot HD-1 bottom wing butting up against the side of the fuselage, the same method of retention as used on the Tiger Moth has worked very well. The top wings join in the centre since there is no centre portion such as on the SE5A. Also the ailerons are mounted in the top wing rather than the bottom wing with the Tiger. When I was building the cabane strut assembly, I epoxied the servo leads to the 10swg wire struts. This was covered with pre-grooved ³⁄₁₆" x ⅜" strip balsa which was epoxied in place and then sanded to an airfoil section. The sockets for the aileron servos came out between the top wings so the plugs from the servos could be connected directly into these. These were arranged to enable the plugs and sockets to be lost within the end of the last plywood wing rib. Two metal strips of 16swg steel ½" wide were cut and epoxied into the wing panel on one side and slots were formed in the other wing rib allowing M4 bolts and T-nuts to be used to retain the wings on th 10swg piano wire.

When I am transporting the wings around or when they are in storage in the workshop I have made up some plywood plates which have 4BA x 1" bolts with nuts let into them. The purpose of these is that the 4BA bolts will go into the brass tubes let into the ends of the wings This allows the wings to be keep in their correct configuration and take a lot of the strain off the inter-wings struts. It also makes the wings far easier to handle without fear of doing damage.

The system which I have just described for all these aircraft seems to be working perfectly well and I am sure that if I designed another bi-plane that lent itself to this method of construction I would certainly use it.

Several modellers have raised the question of how I rig my bi-planes and even after describing this method in some detail to one particular person he came back and told me that his local club "experts" had said that it couldn't be done – sorry to the experts if I have upset them just a little!

If you are about to design or build a bi-plane, it would be well worth considering whether it is possible to use this type of system on your particular model.

Inter Wing Struts

As we have been looking at bi-plane construction in some detail it is worth a look at the inter-wing struts themselves. These are such an important part of the aircraft since they keep the top and bottom wings apart and enable the rigging wires to have something to pull against which makes all the individual units work as a total assembly.

On many aircraft there are a pair of wing struts which have an "X" bracing between them, giving them great rigidity and keeping the wings at their correct incidence.

One of the very simple ways of attaching the wing struts to the spars is to cut out some metal brackets and bend them at approximately 90°. These can be bolted or screwed to the top or bottom wing spar and then a nut and bolt let through the top or bottom of the wing strut and into the bracket. This method would be perfectly functional but wouldn't necessarily do a lot for scale appearance.

The method I have used on the SE5A, Tiger Moth and Hanriot HD-1 is to drill the top and bottom of the inter-wing strut approximately ½" and let in a piece of 6bA or M3 studding. Studding is a continuous length of rod which has been threaded and enables you to cut a piece any length you require. See Fig.31B.

When the studding has been epoxied into the end of the inter wing strut a suitable size hole can be drilled through the wing spars to receive it. When you are assembling this, the studding is pushed up through the wing and a nut is placed on the top to hold it all tightly in place. This system works very well and holds everything very securely in place. The other advantage is that in the event of the aircraft requiring some major repairs it is not too difficult to disassemble the aircraft. If the nuts are recessed under the covering and a small patch applied afterwards, they do not even need to be visible at all.

With the inner-wing struts held in place you will need to fabricate some method of attaching the scale rigging wires. It would be true to say that almost every fullsize aircraft has a slightly different method of attaching the wires.

This is a good example of where plenty of information on the aircraft which you are modelling will help you in deciding the best way of duplicating the fittings. It will help the appearance of the aircraft a great deal as well.

With my Tiger Moth, I worked from documentation and photo when I had to design the attachment points for these wires. I then went to the expense of having the metal fittings laser cut as I am not very fond of metal work! The basic principle could be used for a large number of aircraft with some modification.

The laser cut anchorage points on my Tiger Moth were made specially for me. Also note how the wing strut holds the plate in place.

Chapter 4

Fuselage

One of the most interesting features of scale modelling which appeals not just to me personally but to a lot of other modellers as well is the opportunity to try out different building methods on each new aircraft. Yet one very basic form of fuselage construction keeps on turning up time and time again in totally different types of models. In its most basic form, it will be found in such sport or trainer models as the perennial Super 60.

If you started flying in more recent times with a foam wing trainer then you will have missed out on the open work fuselage with the good old nylon covering and the smell of dope all over the house! The Piper J-3 Super Cub or its variants have a form of fuselage construction which is very similar to the Super 60, in the rear part at least, being made from four longerons with upright and cross members at appropriate spacings. In model form this would be made with ¼" or ⅜" square balsa on a larger model for the longerons and ¼" square for the uprights and cross members with spacing of about three or four inches. As the fuselage in this form would have no rigidity, each rectangle needs to have a brace across it. On most fullsize aircraft the braces are not visible through the covering although it may well be braced with wire or a tubular steel fuselage where the braces would be of a smaller diameter.

Making the brace from ³⁄₁₆" square and fitting it back from the surface will get around this one and a look at Fig.32 gives the rear fuselage in its most basic form (note only two sets of braces have been drawn for clarity).

Building this type of fuselage can be very simple indeed as the individual side can be built directly onto the plan, remembering that you will need to build a right and a left hand side to make a pair. Now is the time to fit any plywood doublers for the wing seat or reinforcing for the engine compartment, a look at Fig.33 will show the general basic arrangement.

The basic fuselage construction for the author's Hanriot HD-1 depicting the longerons with vertical crossmembers plus braces. Also the ply doublers etc. have been fitted to the front of the fuselage.

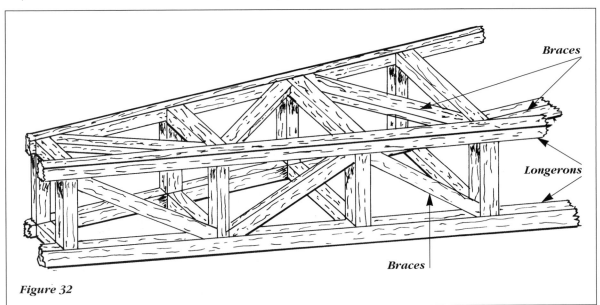

Figure 32

Longerons

Sheet Fill In With ⅟₁₆" Ply Doubler

Figure 33

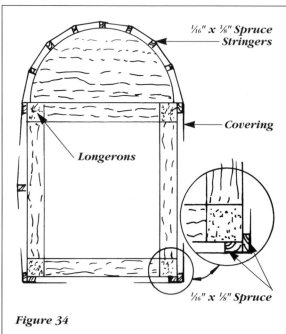

⅟₁₆" x ⅛" Spruce Stringers

Covering

Longerons

⅟₁₆" x ⅛" Spruce

Figure 34

The ⅛" x ⅟₁₆" spruce stringers have been added to the top of the formers in preparation for covering.

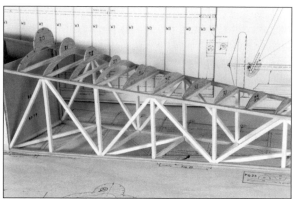

With the addition of formers to the rectangular fuselage the top decking shape can be formed.

Taking this method of fuselage construction a stage further, it is readily adaptable to the WW1 bi-planes with the addition of a half round former cut from ⅛" sheet which can be used to support the stringers to form the top part of the fuselage. If you look at some photos of bi-planes of the period taking the SE5A as an example, no uprights or diagonal braces are visible at all through the covering, only the top and bottom long runs being visible. A way of getting around that little problem is to apply ⅛" x ⅟₁₆" spruce strips to the bottom corners of the fuselage and also to the top longerons as depicted in Fig.34. Another advantage of using the ⅛" x ⅟₁₆" spruce strips glued directly to the longerons is that it will make the model look as if you have used much smaller materials than you have in the actual construction, thereby further enhancing the scale appearance of the finished model.

When it comes to fitting the stringers on top of the fuselage one thing that shows up

more than anything is if you haven't succeeded in getting those stringers dead straight. Nothing looks worse than wavy stringers! Personally I only notch the stringers into the first former and sometimes at the rear of the fuselage. The intermediate formers I leave at a slightly smaller size and glue the stringers directly to the top of the former. You can see that this gives me the opportunity, when I am gluing the stringers in place, to use a straight edge and make sure the stringers are in exactly the right place when pinning. If the notches have been one hundred percent accurate the stringers finish up looking dead straight.

One other point worth remembering at this stage is that most of the joints in this type of construction are really no more than end grain butted against another piece of wood which, in woodworking terms, is hardly regarded as a joint at all. You are therefore rather dependant on the glue you use being strong and having flexibility in it. I would always use one of the white PVA glues rather than balsa cement or Superglue which both tend to be a little on the rigid side.

The next type of fuselage which uses this basic method of construction is the all stringer type fuselage, the method I used to make the rear portion of my Avro Anson fuselage. With the addition of four semi-circular pieces of ⅛" sheet a complete former can be made up using very little balsa indeed. A look at Fig.35A shows what I mean and you will note that I have not notched the stringers into the former, again allowing me to keep the stringers running straight as previously mentioned. This way the former will not show through the covering in a non-scale position allowing the modeller to choose where he wishes to put the formers rather than being dictated to by where the fullsize aircraft formers were located.

When I had the opportunity to photograph the fullsize Avro Anson which I based the model on I noticed that the fuselage stringers were only something like 1" x ½" spruce which is quite small when you think that you are going to reduce them to a scale model size. To make the stringers on the model appear slim I used ¹⁄₁₆" x ⅛" spruce. By using spruce I managed to maintain a reasonable degree of strength without incurring a great weight penalty. When you consider that there are only four longerons running the full length of the fuselage the spruce stringers and the uprights with bracing plus a very small amount of ⅛" sheet for balsa, it is easy to realise just how lightly the rear part of the fuselage can be built. This is all important when it comes to saving weight at the rear to get the

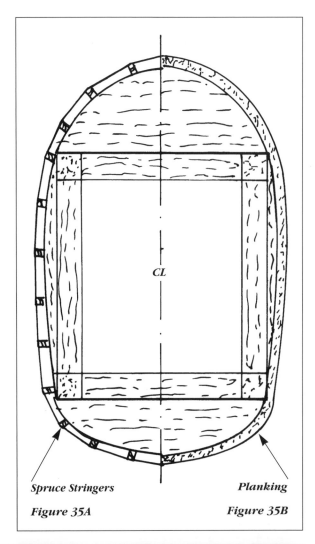

Spruce Stringers

Planking

Figure 35A

Figure 35B

The basic fuselage construction for your author's 1/4 scale SE5A with the glassfibre top decking alongside.

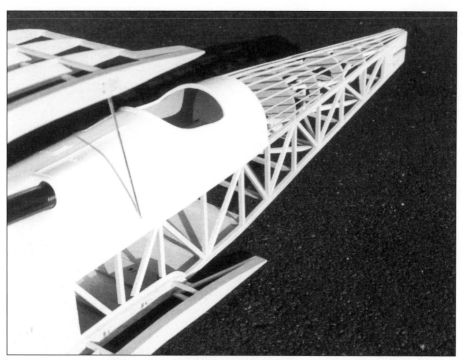

The rear of the SE5A fuselage with glassfibre top decking in place plus the rear formers and spruce stringers attached.

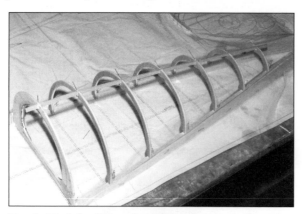

Top half of the Miles Gemini fuselage is built with the longerons pinned directly to the plan and then the half formers added to that.

The two rear halves of the Miles Gemini fuselage awaiting being stuck together. This clearly shows the accessibility you have for fitting any components within the fuselage.

centre of gravity in the right position. To demonstrate the versatility of this method of construction, using the same method to form the fuselage formers, the model can now in fact be planked in its entirety with ⅛" or ³⁄₃₂" sheet for a smaller model and you can finish up with a fuselage which would be suitable for a WW2 fighter. Fig.35B shows the all planked fuselage detail which certainly shows that this basic construction method is extremely versatile going from something like a Spitfire through to a Piper Cub, not forgetting the WW1 type planes on the way!

The construction of the Westland Lysander is fairly interesting being panelled at the front and rear and having stringers with fabric covering in the middle. The basic internal fuselage consists of ¼" square longerons with ¼" square verticals, uprights and braces. With the basic internal structure of longerons etc. made up, it only required small segments to be applied at the appropriate former positions for complete formers to be made up, which was extremely economical on balsa, only requiring one sheet to complete the entire fuselage.

To achieve the different type of external appearance, the front and rear parts of the fuselage were planked with ⅛" sheet balsa to give the smooth finish required in preparation for the simulation of the metal panel work at a later stage. With contrasting methods of construction like this you never quite know where to put the fuselage formers so that they support the end of the sheet or are in the right place to support the end of the stringers. The method I finally decided to use was to mount the formers in such a position that they lined up with the end of the sheeting. That could then be positioned very easily and to get the stringers in the right place I simply cut some notches into the ⅛" sheeting the right size and spacing to take the ⅛" x ¹⁄₁₆" spruce stringers. It is useful to mark the positions where the stringers are going onto the formers having taken this information from the plan which then gave me the correct positions for the stringers. As the positions are fixed at the back and front of the aircraft only you can now glue the stringers in place making sure that you have them straight by using a straight edge.

As the Lysander canopy is rather large and will make viewing of the inside of the aircraft fairly easy when the model is complete, I had to make sure it looked the part even if there was a pilot and passenger to block some of the view. I decided it would be worth painting the inside of the fuselage before it was covered and even before the spruce stringers were applied so that the simulated metal parts could be painted the light interior green which seems to have been so popular on this era of aircraft. The idea here was that when the stringers were applied they would be left their natural colour and when the covering was applied it would be left the natural linen colour so that it would show correctly on the inside of the cockpit. Trying to paint the interior once the aircraft was built would have proved extremely difficult to achieve anything like a reasonable finish.

Lower half of the Miles Gemini fuselage with part of the planking already in place. The curved portion was pre-soaked and held in position with tape and allowed to dry. It was then removed before being glued in place with the curve pre-formed in it.

Fuselage Construction In Two Halves

I have already described a fuselage construction system where you use longerons with vertical and cross members for braces. This is followed by applying formers to make the required fuselage section after which the entire fuselage can be planked. The initial stages of this construction can be completed on a flat building board but after that it will need to be built clear of the board.

An alternative method is to build the top and bottom half of the fuselage separately. See Fig.36. Before you can start building this way you will need to decide on a convenient line down the side of the fuselage. On some aircraft there will be a convenient point such as the edge of the cockpit frame which will be parallel with the datum line. Project this line through to the back and

front of the aircraft and see whether it is in a convenient place at both ends of the fuselage. Alternatively draw a line parallel with the datum line that will give you roughly equal amounts of fuselage above and below your line.

When you cut out your fuselage formers mark the vertical centre line and the new horizontal split line. After the formers have been cut ready for building they will all need cutting in half on the horizontal line. You will also need to make a cutout in each side of the former to accept a ⅛" x ¼" balsa longeron. You may now cut out any other notches that will be required later in the construction as well.

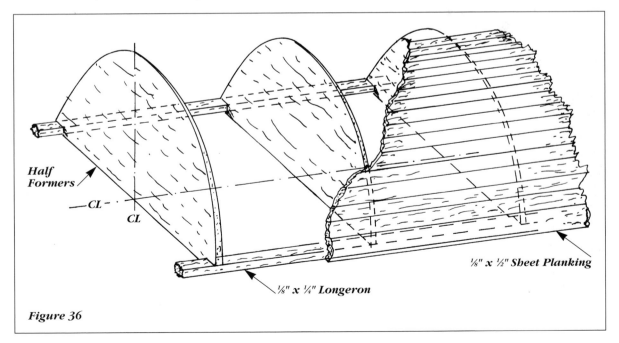

Half Formers

— CL -

CL

⅛" x ¼" *Longeron*

⅛" x ½" *Sheet Planking*

Figure 36

You will now need to make up ⅛" x ¼" balsa longerons which are sufficiently long to go from one end of the fuselage to the other. When you have four of these, two will need placing on the plan far enough from the edge of the fuselage to allow for the sheeting which will be applied to the fuselage later. With the longerons in place, all the top fuselage formers can be stuck into their correct position, making sure they are vertical. Allow the glue to dry thoroughly before you start planking the top half of the fuselage.

If there is only a gentle curve to the fuselage you can cut strips as wide as you can and apply these. Where the curve of the fuselage will not allow this then you will need to plank with much narrower strips – typically half an inch wide.

When you have completed the top half of the fuselage construction it may now be removed from the building board. Again you will need to fasten the balsa longerons over the plan and stick the bottom half fuselage formers to the longerons. Before you start planking the fuselage there will be some ply doublers over the wing seat to be fitted along with any strengthening points for undercarriages etc. When all these parts have been fitted you can plank the bottom of the fuselage as already described for the top. Let the glue thoroughly dry before removing the bottom half of the fuselage from the plan. The top and bottom half of the fuselage can be offered up to each other just to double check that you have the correct fit for the two halves.

Before you glue the top and bottom halves together you may wish to fit components whilst you still have good access to them and add cockpit detail as well. You may also be able to build the tailplane into one part of the fuselage before placing the second half into position, thereby trapping the tailplane.

If the fuselage you are working on is going to be for a single engined aircraft the firewall would have to be cut in half as well. Assuming you were intending to use ¼" ply for the firewall the alternative would be to cut two firewalls from ⅛" ply and cut one of these in half. The two half components would be built into the fuselage during its construction but would be set back on the rear line for the firewall. When the two halves of the fuselage are subsequently glued together down their join lines there would be nothing to stop you gluing the uncut ⅛" ply firewall in place now. This would give you the almost identical continuity of strength that you would have expected from the ¼" ply firewall.

Obviously this system of construction is only suitable for a fully sheeted fuselage but has many advantages. Firstly you can build directly over the plan pinning everything to the building board which will keep it very rigid. By building this way your fuselage will finish up straight and accurate (or as accurate as your building will allow!). Also, having two halves will enable you to gain access to any internal parts such as retracting tailwheels etc. which can be fitted in the bottom half of the fuselage before the top part is finally glued in place and a lot of cockpit detail can be completed with good access to the lower half of the fuselage.

The author's 1/4 scale Sirocco features very simple fuselage construction using the slab sider technique with the one piece of glassfibre moulding which is stuck directly to the top of the fuselage.

When the two halves of the fuselage have been completed, the centre portion of the fuselage formers can be cut away to save weight which is particularly important towards the rear of the fuselage. Also of course you have no internal structure such as quarter square longerons which will save weight as well. I used this system of construction very successfully on my Czechoslovakian Moravia L200D twin aircraft and the Miles Gemini twin.

Finally, when the two halves of the fuselage are stuck together, you can give the entire fuselage a good sanding to blend in the top and bottom halves and all the planking etc.

Sheet Sided Fuselages

The all sheet or slab side fuselage construction is very common on sport models but does not lend itself too often to scale aircraft. Two aircraft which I have designed over the years and which lend themselves well to this method of construction are the Miles Magister and the Sirocco. The Magister has flat sides which can be cut from sheet with half inch triangular blocks applied to the bottom of the fuselage and then ³⁄₃₂" sheet applied across the bottom. When this had dried the bottom corner can then be sanded to give a nice rounded appearance to the model. The top of the fuselage will need planking into the tops of the formers. See Fig.37.

My original 57" span Sirocco used all sheet fuselage sides fitted to the fuselage formers to give the side of the fuselage a bit of shape. The bottom of this fuselage was planked with ³⁄₃₂" as the aircraft had square corners.

The top of the fuselage was then planked which generated quite a bit of work on this small aircraft. Subsequently I built a larger version at quarter scale which has a wing span of 69". The same method was used for the fuselage sides and the bottom as on the previous model.

On the larger Sirocco I made a complete glassfibre top decking which was then fitted directly to the top edge of the sides. With this method of construction the curved top decking is a very easy item to fit on the larger model and a great improvement over the planking of the smaller one. An alternative method is to use an internal sheet frame to which you can apply ⅛" x ⅛" stringers (or slightly larger) to produce the outside shape of the aircraft. This would be particularly useful where the entire fuselage is fabric covered and will only need stringers to show through the covering at the appropriate points. See Fig.38, which shows this method of construction which was used very successfully on my Laser 200 design.

Plywood Reinforcement

As already mentioned, plywood doublers will be fitted to the fuselage over the wing seat and ply will also be used for the firewall. There will probably be plywood used to fix the undercarriage if this is mounted to the fuselage. In the interests of trying to keep a model as light as you can, it is best to avoid the use of large lumps of heavy plywood. Whilst designing a scale model, if I can possibly make one piece of plywood

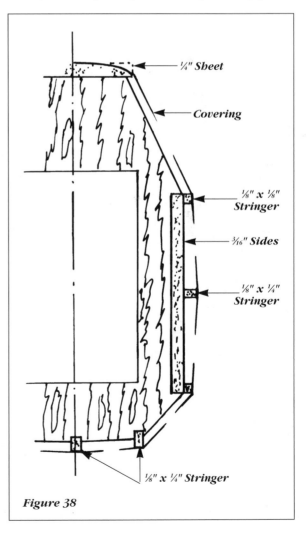

¼" Sheet

Covering

⅛" x ⅛" Stringer

³⁄₁₆" Sides

⅛" x ¼" Stringer

⅛" x ¼" Stringer

Figure 38

⅛" Sheet Planking

³⁄₁₆" Sides

³⁄₃₂" Sheeting

½" Triangle

Figure 37

This photo is of the fullsize SE5A with the covering removed to reveal lightweight construction particularly for the rear end of the fuselage. Note the bracing wires to give this lightweight construction greater rigidity.

perform two functions I certainly will. If you can avoid using plywood behind the centre of gravity it is also a very good idea, as of course you will almost certainly have to add lead to the nose of the aircraft to balance it out at a later stage. Even keeping the weight down in front of the centre of gravity can be a good idea because it allows you to carry a larger NiCad pack rather than wasting weight with lead or heavy pieces of plywood. It is also worth deciding whether you really need to use ¼" ply or whether ⅛" ply would do just as well. Items such as the firewall could always have a piece of ½" x ¼" spruce glued across the back of it which would increase its rigidity quite considerably with a very small increase in weight.

The ply doublers to the fuselage at the sides can also be cut away or generally reduced in size if they are made from ¹⁄₁₆" ply – on smaller models it might be quite practical to use ¹⁄₃₂" ply.

All plywoods that you intend to use in areas that require strength will need to be birch faced ply which is a good quality, strong product. If you wish to use a large ply former for example in an area where it does not needs to be particularly strong, lite ply would be a very good alternative.

As the name implies, it is considerably lighter than a normal birch ply so can be used for such items as formers without a vast increase in weight but would still be a little heavier than the balsa equivalent. If you are looking for a little greater strength over balsa then this would be a very useful alternative. If the ply former is to have anything bolted to it then lite ply is not particularly suit-

able as it crushes quite easily so do be selective in its use.

.4mm ply has already been mentioned in wing construction and is useful for strengthening parts of the fuselage with very little weight gain. On my Miles Gemini twin I wished to have very light fuselage formers which I could subsequently cut down to reduce weight. As I was building the fuselage in two halves as already described I wished to have panels sufficiently large to cut the formers from one piece of wood. The method I used was to butt joint some sheets of ⅛" balsa to produce a sufficiently wide piece for the formers. Then I stuck .4mm ply to each side of the balsa using contact adhesive such as Evostick Impact. The largest former was cut first and then the inside of it was cut away leaving the former only ⅜" wide. Conveniently, on the Gemini rear fuselage, it tapers at a constant rate allowing you to cut every other former from the off-cut of the previous piece. So with just two sheets of balsa/ply laminate all the formers could be cut. By using ⅛" balsa in the centre it gave the former some thickness and kept the .4mm ply sufficiently far apart to give this some structural rigidity.

When the fuselage top and bottom halves were finally glued together this resulted in a very light but strong construction and will certainly have many useful applications in the future.

On a slightly lighter hearted note it is interesting that we build our models with balsa which is of course a hardwood and to reinforce them we use plywood which is a softwood!

Chapter 5

Fixing Glassfibre Cowls and Engine Compartments

Almost every fullsize aircraft has some form of cowling to conceal or partly conceal the engine that is used to power the aircraft. With the tremendous variety of engines used within fullsize aircraft, the cowl shapes will be many and varied. The cowl is kept as small as it can be in the interests of streamlining so it will fairly snugly fit the fullsize engine.

The early WW1 aircraft were powered by rotary engines and this of course is the reason for the traditional circular spun aluminium cowl. In most model aircraft kits this is exactly what the scale modeller will be offered for the front of his aircraft. An obvious exception to this would be the SE5A which had no cowl as such and access to the engine is via a removable top panel. On later aircraft the cowl shape would vary considerably from this as the single row rotary engine was replaced by in-line or "V" multi-cylinder engines. This then result-

ed in a much longer and slimmer cowl which greatly improved the aerodynamics of the aircraft. In most cases, if you are buying a kit or working from a scale plan, there will be a glassfibre cowl available to you. If you are a scratch builder, however, you may wish to make a glassfibre cowl for yourself although on a one-off basis this is a lot of expensive and hard work. Alternatively you may be able to make your cowl from balsa depending on the shape.

One thing which is almost certain is that on any of the later aircraft that had in-line engines the cowl will be a lot longer from the front to the firewall than our model engine will require. If the cowl is far longer than the model engine on its engine mount, one solution would be to get an extremely long engine mount but this may not be available commercially and will not be a satisfactory answer to the problem in any case. The far better

The front of your author's 1/4 scale Tiger Moth clearly shows the engine box which was used to position the engine mount in the correct place.

The glassfibre cowl removed on the author's quarter scale Tiger Moth to reveal the accessibility you have to the engine compartment.

of fuel they will not go into the fuselage. Also by removing the cowl you have complete access to the engine as well as the front of the fuel tank if you need to inspect the clunk or the plumbing at any stage. These are all important considerations if you are to have a practical flying model which you can maintain and keep reliable for a number of years.

I have used quarter ply to build the boxes up and it is best if a pair of slots are cut into the firewall so that the side plates can be let-in to the firewall and firmly glued in place. The front of the box, where it joins the side plates, is best formed if some form of inter-locking joint is used as this will vastly increase the strength over a butt joint however well it may be glued. If, on the top or bottom of the box, you use a piece of 1/16" ply this will give the whole box a considerable increase in rigidity but its position will very much depend on whether you place the fuel tank at the top or bottom and whether receivers, NiCads or servos are also to go in there. See Fig.39. This illustrates the box arrangement which I have used very successfully on my quarter scale Tiger Moth which is powered by a 120 OS 4-stroke motor.

If you are building a kit you would expect all these parts to be cut for you and the side plates left a little on the longer side to give you some adjustment to suit different engine installations.

alternative is to build a box onto the front of the firewall which can then have the engine mount fastened in the correct place to suit our model engine requirements. I have used this basic system on a number of aircraft over the years and found it extremely satisfactory. An added advantage is that the fuel tank can be built into the box as well. The benefits of this are that the fuel tank is kept within the engine compartment so if there are any leaks

Fixing Glassfibre Cowls

Many modellers seem to think that to fix a glassfibre cowl you need do nothing more than glue some hardwood blocks to the engine firewall and then screw through the cowl to retain it. Invariably you find with this method that the screw holes enlarge very

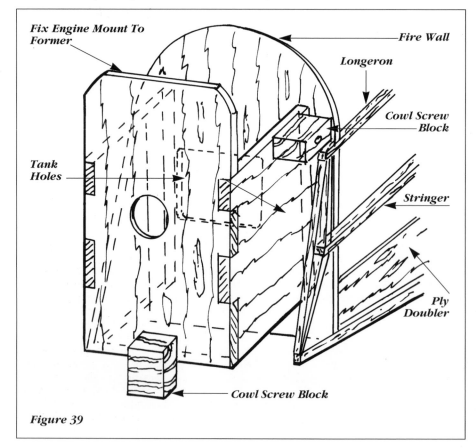

Fix Engine Mount To Former

Fire Wall

Longeron

Cowl Screw Block

Tank Holes

Stringer

Ply Doubler

Cowl Screw Block

Figure 39

quickly to such a point that the heads of the screws will go through the hole. The next standard modification is to then fit large washers and you can imagine that it doesn't take very long before the hole gets even larger. What needs to be remembered here is that the cowl is getting shaken by the vibration from the engine and also that there is probably fuel and oil been thrown around the inside of the cowl all of which does nothing to help the fixing of the cowl to the fuselage. The method I have used very successfully on a number of my models in recent years is as shown in Fig.40. The firewall of the aircraft has a rebate built into it from ¼" square balsa which has the effect of holding the glassfibre cowl securely in its correct position. You should arrange the balsa so that it will be a snug fit within the cowl. At convenient points around the cowl you will need to let in pieces of hardwood roughly half an inch square by an inch long. These can be pieces of beech which are sold as engine bearer stock in model shops and can be

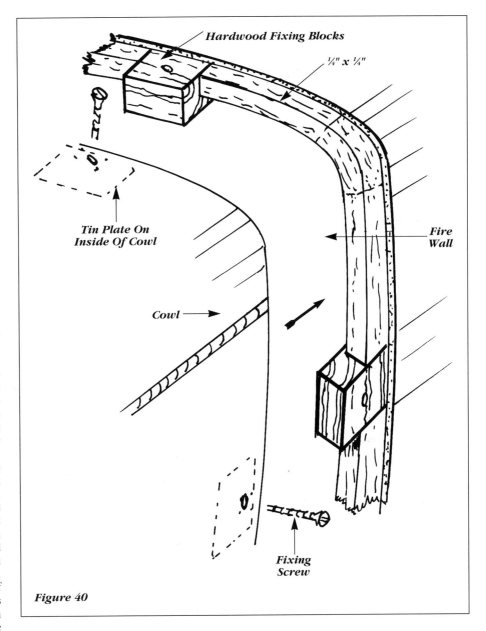

Hardwood Fixing Blocks

¼" x ¼"

Tin Plate On Inside Of Cowl

Cowl →

Fire Wall

Fixing Screw

Figure 40

a useful material for a number of applications. The idea of building the rebate is so the cowl will be held firmly in place all the way round and the screws are left to do little more than to stop the cowl actually sliding off the front of the aircraft.

The second thing which is well worth doing is to cut pieces of tin plate roughly one inch square and glassfibre these to the inside of the cowl. If you have tin cans left over from the kitchen these can be cut into pieces of flat metal. Try and avoid the tin cans which have the corrugation around the middle although there are still a number of cans these days which have a reasonable amount of flat metal on them. Decide where the screws are going to go through the cowl and then mix up some polyester resin so that the piece of tin plate can be stuck in place and then, with some woven cloth, put this over the metal. Thoroughly soak this in and allow to set. As the glassfibre leaves the manufacturing process, the surface will have some rough spots on it but far more importantly little will want to stick to it, so it is well

worth going over the areas that you intend to glassfibre with some very coarse sandpaper to break down the surface and roughen it up. If you have any glassfibre resin cleaner (usually acetone or cellulose thinners) these should also be brushed onto the areas and allowed to dry before you start glassfibring. When you have the tin plate and glassfibre patches on the inside of the cowl in place and it has had at least 24 hours to fully cure, you should drill the correct size hole to suit the screws you are intending to use. These holes should be countersunk to fit the screws you are using. It is very important to use countersunk screws as each time you refit the cowl and tighten the screws the countersink will pull into the tin plate hole and keep it tight. This may seem a little more work than is really necessary but I have found that by using this method the screw holes do not enlarge so it is well worth the extra effort. At the time of writing my Tiger Moth, which has the cowl fitted this way, has achieved over seventy flights and the holes are showing no sign of enlarging.

Chapter 6

Attaching Fixed Undercarriages

Most early aircraft had fairly narrow tracked undercarriages which were designed for flying off grass. These were invariably fixed directly to the fuselages as the wings of the period had only sufficient strength to withstand flying loads. With aircraft flying from tarmac runways coupled with improved design, wider track undercarriages became the norm. Many of these wider track undercarriages were fitted directly to the wing whether they were of the fixed or retracing variety. We will look first at the earlier type of undercarriage which is fixed directly to the fuselage.

Typical of this configuration is the WW1 bi-plane that also had quite large diameter wheels which were designed for flying off the grass airfields of the period. Nowadays as a number of the former RAF airfields have been lost to the use of aeromodellers many pilots are now flying from a grass flying strip. This type of undercarriage works very well for a model with the large diameter slim wheels which cut through the grass very

The author's 1/4 scale Tiger Moth undercarriage with the balsa cladding in place and scale detail added to it. Lithoplate has been added to the undercarriage fairings to enhance their scale appearance.

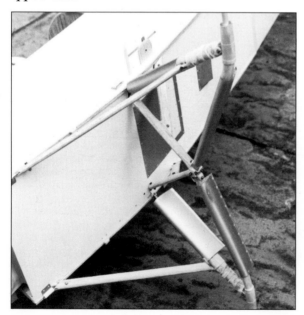

well. The taildragger configuration also allows you to get sufficient angle of attack on the model and lift off easily where the tricycle undercarriage can be a problem under some weather conditions.

On bi-planes in general there always seems to be a certain amount of discussion as to whether the undercarriage should be sprung or left solid. The advantages of a sprung undercarriage are that when the model lands some of the forces at the moment of contact with the ground will be absorbed by the undercarriage springing and not transferred to the model. Most of the WW1 fighters did not have oleo type legs which came later but had bungee cord wrapped around the axles to give a degree of springing. This is quite easy to duplicate in model form as small diameter bungee cord can be obtained from ships chandlers.

The biggest disadvantage I have experienced with sprung undercarriages on bi-planes is under windy conditions. On a windy day a bi-plane will catch the wind whilst it is on the ground and will blow over if given half a chance. This situation can be greatly aggravated if the springing in the undercarriage is allowing the model to rock thereby allowing the wind to get under the tips even more easily. Personally I have always gone for a solid undercarriage, relying on the tyre of the wheel to take any landing loads and this seems to have worked perfectly well. With the undercarriage being that much

The undercarriage structure used on the author's quarter scale Hanriot HD-1.

more solid, on a windy day the aircraft is less likely to blow around on the ground and during take-off and landing. You may find your bi-plane is perfectly easy to fly on a windy day but the difficult times are take-off or landing and that is when damage is most likely to be sustained.

The proof in my mind that you do not need a sprung undercarriage to save damage to the model is borne out by the fact that my SE5A has had well over 110 flights with many touch and go's and no damage to the under-carriage has yet occurred. My Tiger Moth also has a solid undercarriage. I admit all my flying is done from run-ways but perhaps these are less forgiving in the event of a hard landing than a grass strip. If you fly regularly from rough grass, some suspension in the undercarriage might be beneficial to save wear and tear. The trade off against this of course would be that on a windy day the model may get blown over but the final choice is yours.

The main undercarriage leg and rear strut on my SE5A are cut from ¼" sheet spruce. See Fig.41. These two parts are glued together at the axle fairing but to increase the strength of this joint a saw cut is made down the middle of the two pieces. When this has been done a piece of ⅟₁₆" ply can be glued into the slot to reinforce the area.

On the Hanriot HD-1 the legs on the fullsize aircraft are of an airfoil section and appear to be made from metal tube. To simulate this I made mine from ¾" x ⅜" spruce sanded to section. Where the main and rear leg meet I have a laser cut plate which the axle is fitted into. This axle plate is fitted by cutting a pair of slots in the bottom end of the spruce legs and it is then epoxied into its correct position. Where the legs are fitted to the underside of the fuselage exactly the same method has been used on both aircraft. One inch by ¼" ply strips have been fitted across the fuselage and let into the ply fuselage doublers. See Fig.42. The advantage of fixing these plates firmly into the doublers is that the loads from landing will be spread over a far wider area of the model than purely onto the ply plate itself. To attach the legs to the ply plate I cut 16swg by ½" wide mild steel sheet to form an angle bracket which could then be fitted to the bottom of the fuse-lage with 6BA nuts and bolts. The other part of the bracket then pro-truded below the fuse-lage. Slots are cut in the tops of the undercar-riage legs and attached with nuts and bolts. This system seems to have worked very well on my aircraft so far!

The undercarriage on the Tiger Moth is a somewhat different proposition altogether. The main frame for that is bent from 6 and 10swg piano wire. When all the parts had been cut and bent they

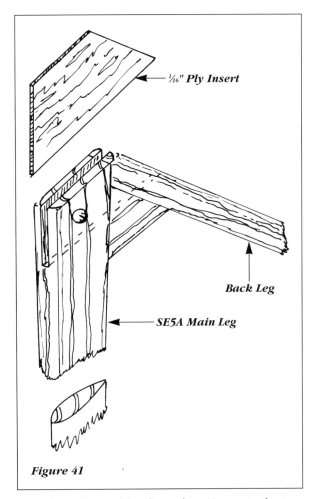

Figure 41

were then silver soldered together. To create the true scale appearance of the undercarriage, two pieces of wood which had been pre-grooved to accept the 6 or 10swg piano wire were epoxied to either side of the

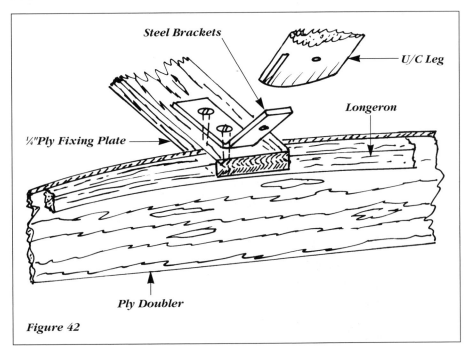

Figure 42

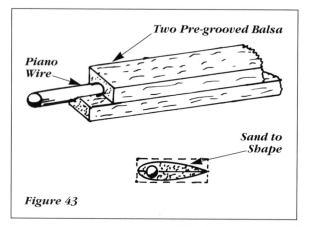

Figure 43

Two Pre-grooved Balsa

Piano Wire

Sand to Shape

undercarriage legs. See Fig.43. When this was subsequently sanded to an airfoil section and with a little extra detail, the illusion of a true sprung undercarriage could be created very easily. On the Tiger Moth the main oleos appear to go into attachments within the fuselage. The main legs were made from one piece of 6swg wire which formed both axles and legs and went across the fuselage underside. The main attachment point was recessed within the fuselage floor. A piece of 1" x ¼" ply was let in across the bottom of the fuselage and recessed into the ¹⁄₁₆" ply doublers. The legs were held in place on the ply block using aluminium saddles which could be located in position with nuts and bolts. This has proved very reliable in operation.

These basic systems could be used on many aircraft of this period with only slight modifications to suit the actual aircraft type. My Westland Lysander, on the other hand, has a very distinctive undercarriage which is built into the fuselage and the method of building this was totally different to the WW1 type of undercarriage. The first part I made was the glassfibre wheel spats for the main lower part which proved very durable in operation. The main functional part of the undercarriage was made from a piece of 6swg wire which was bolted to a ply plate let into the bottom of the fuselage and attached to the ply doublers. This main leg was bent down and bent again to form the axles. Parallel to the main leg was a secondary one made from 10swg and kept as far apart as it could to give the greatest structural rigidity. This leg was also bent down from the fuselage but joined the 6swg leg before that was bent to form the axle. At this point both legs were bound and soft soldered to keep them in their true position. Fig.44 depicts the basic piano wire structure of this undercarriage. The parallel part of the upper leg which butts up against the side of the fuselage was clad with quarter sheet balsa top and bottom which had been grooved to

The De Havilland Tiger Moth undercarriage complete, further enhanced with a pair of realistic wheels for the aircraft.

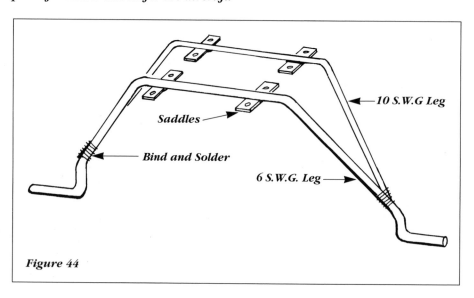

Figure 44

Saddles

Bind and Solder

10 S.W.G Leg

6 S.W.G. Leg

accommodate the 6 and 10swg piano wire. This was epoxied into position and then sanded to an airfoil section. The lower portion of this was rebated away a little so that it would accept the glassfibre wheel spats which were glassfibred in place. The balsa was then blended in to the glassfibre in preparation for covering. As the main legs could bend a little the balsa was taken very close to the fuselage side covering but did not actually touch it to allow for flexing.

On some of the more modern aircraft such as the Cessna 150 range, the undercarriage is made from nothing more sophisticated than a single piece of aluminium cut and bent to the desired shape. This aluminium of course would be one of the better grades on the fullsize aircraft but to simulate it in model form you would use the identical system whilst being very careful about the selection of grade of aluminium for the job.

An alternative to aluminium these days seems to be carbon fibre and epoxy resin. To make an undercarriage this way you would entail the making of a suitable mould which might be beyond the skills and expertise of some modellers. Both the aluminium and the carbon fibre undercarriages are commercially available to suit certain aircraft types and by the time both of these systems have been given a coat of paint they would be indistinguishable from one another. Fig.45 illustrates this type of undercarriage where it has become very common practice to use a cap head bolt and nut as the axle for the wheel.

Fixed undercarriages on wings can fall into two or three categories. The first is basically the type using aluminium or carbon fibre, as just described for a Cessna 150 type aircraft but instead of being fixed to the fuselage, it could just as easily be fixed to the forward portion of the centre wing. In the earlier part of this book I described the fixing for torsion bar undercarriages within foam core wings and the attendant problems attached to that. With a built-up wing it is far easier to incorporate this type of undercarriage. Fig.46 gives the general arrangement for this system.

The undercarriage for the Westland Lysander with the glassfibre wheelspats awaiting fixing.

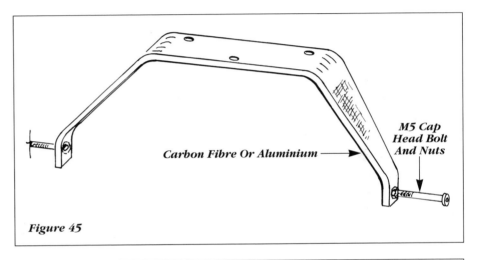

Carbon Fibre Or Aluminium

M5 Cap Head Bolt And Nuts

Figure 45

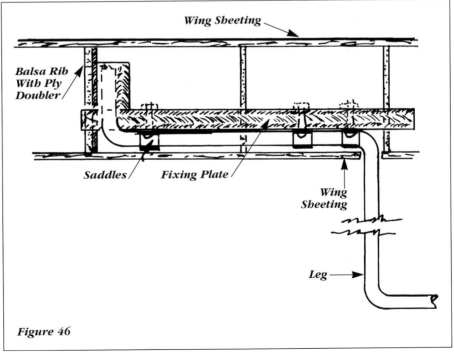

Wing Sheeting

Balsa Rib With Ply Doubler

Saddles   *Fixing Plate*

Wing Sheeting

Leg

Figure 46

Firstly you need to position your piece of 1" wide x ¼" ply a sufficient distance from the bottom wing skin to comfortably clear your undercarriage leg and retaining saddles. Before you build the wing you will need to decide which wing ribs this ply fixing plate will come in contact with and attach ⅟₁₆" ply doublers to spread the load. These doublers will be strongest if started from the leading edge, taking in the main spars and travelling at least as far as the mid point of the rib. If there are rear spars built into the wing then take the doublers back and attach them there as well. When you have built the wing you can let in the ¼" x 1" wide ply into the slots you have cut in the ribs.

You will also need to cut a short piece of ply to retain the end of the torque rod which will need firmly gluing against the side of the rib. All this work will need to be completed before bolting the leg in place using two or preferably three saddles of the correct size to hold the leg securely.

When that has been completed the bottom wing sheeting can be glued in place with an oval slot cut in it to accept the leg. The slot will of course need to be oval as the leg will move backwards and forwards to accept the loads on landing.

In the days when I used to fly aerobatic models which had this type of undercarriage – but of the slightly more functional and visible variety featuring 8swg legs – there were several occasions when what appeared to be perfectly good landings resulted in the tyre going back sufficiently far to leave a black mark on the underside of the wing skinning! That perhaps illustrates the amount of punishment this type of undercarriage can soak up without failing but also indicates the type of loads that you are putting on an undercarriage as well!

The undercarriage leg may have some form of oleo or streamlined fairing on it and this can be applied once the wing skinning has been completed. It is also worth remembering to leave sufficient gap between it and the wing skinning to allow the leg to bend back. If you do not it will bend in any case

The finished undercarriage on the Hanriot HD-1. Note there is very functional bracing wires and also the simulated bungee cord on this unsprung undercarriage.

the first time you land and possibly result in your wing skinning being split. This type of torsion bar undercarriage can be fitted to many aircraft with only slight modifications to the basic principle.

If your aircraft is a low wing aircraft and fitted with some form of spat which covers the entire leg along with the top half of the wheel you can still use the torsion bar undercarriage. One thing that you may have a problem with is on landing when the leg bends backwards and could well do quite a bit of damage within the spat. The modification to this would be to fit a rear ¼" x 1" ply fixing plate parallel with the main one and then fit a rear strut which is attached to the main leg.

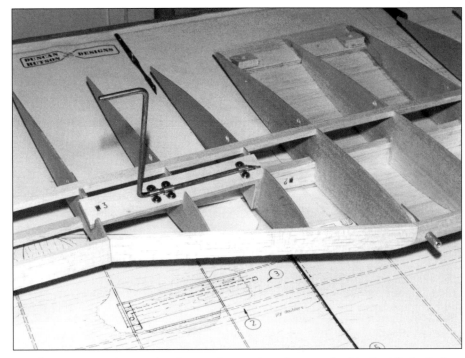

The 6swg piano wire torsion bar undercarriage leg attached to the ¼" ply fixing plates before the wing skinning was fitted to the quarter scale Sirocco.

This would need binding with fuse wire and soft soldering in place. When the undercarriage has been complete the wheel can be fixed in place and, as access to it is going to be extremely limited once the spat is complete, a secure fixing for the wheel is highly recommended.

Over the years I have used brass collets which are screwed in place but found them a bit lacking in performance. Nowadays I much prefer to soft solder washers on both sides of the wheels even if this is a slightly tricky operation. To date I have never had a wheel come off with soldered washers.

With the wheel fixed in place the spat can now be assembled each side of the leg using glassfibre resin and cloth within the spat. To stick the spat to the wheel skinning I have found silicone rubber to be the best. This can be a very good adhesive but it also remains slightly flexible allowing the spat to move without breaking – important

since there will be quite a bit of punishment handed out to the undercarriage on landing. Fig.47 illustrates the spatted undercarriage with the additional rear brace.

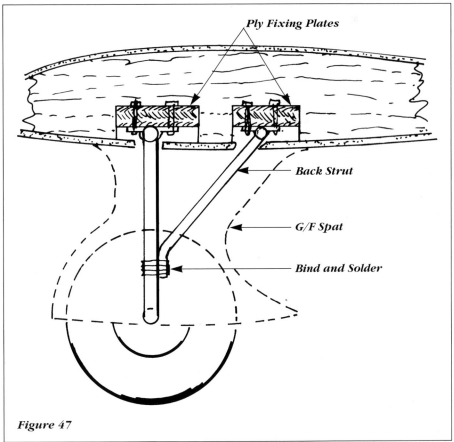

Ply Fixing Plates

Back Strut

G/F Spat

Bind and Solder

Figure 47

Chapter 7

Tailplanes, Fins and Rudder Construction

The tailplane and elevator have a very pronounced effect on the flying qualities of an aircraft. If the tailplane is too small you will have difficulty in making the aircraft sufficiently stable in model form and if the distance between the tailplane and the trailing edge of the wing is comparatively small that will do little to help stability. Ideally what we are looking for is a tailplane which is mounted a reasonable distance away from the trailing edge of the wing. An ideal ratio is 1.2 to 1.5 times the cord of the wing. The further the tailplane is away from the wing the greater the leverage effect it has in stabilising the pitch of the aircraft so that a small tailplane on a long fuselage would be the equal of a larger one on a shorter fuselage. The size of the elevator will also have an effect on the aircraft's flight performance when you consider that if the aircraft gets into a steep dive the only way of getting it out will be by using the elevator to remedy the situation to avoid disastrous consequences.

Fins and rudder on the other hand have a less important effect on the flying characteristics ,providing they are of sufficient area to avoid the aircraft going into a side slip situation at low speed. This can be a bit of a problem on some of the earlier aircraft but is generally not a problem at all on the later designs. Many aircraft feature very distinctive fin and rudder shapes and none more distinctive perhaps than that of the De Havilland range of aircraft or the Spitfire. It is important when you are building the aircraft to try and keep the rear end of your model as light as possible. As the tailplane etc. is a long way behind the centre of gravity a small build up of weight will need a lot of weight at the front to balance out the aircraft!

My favourite method of constructing tailplanes, fins, rudders and elevators if they are to be fabric covered is to use the centre membrane technique. This basically consists of cutting a piece of ⅟₁₆" sheet the size of the tailplane or control surface that is to be modelled. By applying half ribs to the top and bottom with leading edge and trailing edges built the same way you have the basic structure. The trailing edge is made from ⅛" x ¼" or ¼" x ¼" top and bottom with the leading edge being ⅛" x ¼" or ⅛" x ⅛". Corners can be cut from ⅛" sheet and glued in place top and bottom. Fig.48 gives you a general idea how to build this type of tailplane. The building sequence for this is to glue up the necessary sheets of ⅟₁₆" sheet to cut the tailplane from and then pin this to the plan on a flat building board. You may now glue the leading edge and curved pieces to the top of the tailplane and pin in position. Now the half ribs and riblets can be

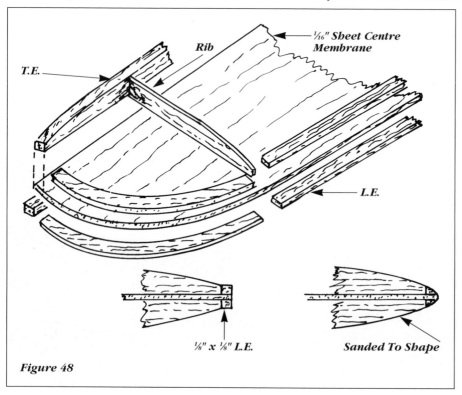

Figure 48

glued in place. Finally the ⅛" x ¼" or ¼" x ¼" trailing edge can be glued in place.

When the glue has thoroughly dried you can unpin the structure from the building board and repeat the process on the other side. When the second lot of glue has thoroughly dried you can sand the leading edge to a round section to represent that of your prototype. Give the whole structure a light sanding and it is then ready for covering.

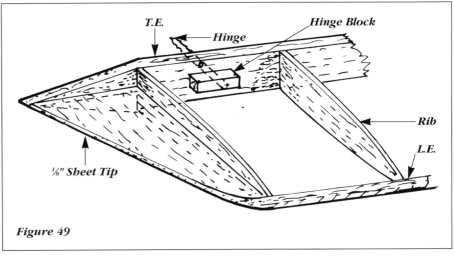

Figure 49

By using fairly slim materials around the edges it will simulate the internal structure of an early bi-plane very effectively. If you are determined to save every ounce you may wish to cut some lightening holes in the ¹⁄₁₆" sheet centre membrane but do not do it to the point where you are reducing the strength of this component. This method of construction is ideally suited to the fin as well whilst the elevators and rudder would require a slimmer trailing edge made typically from ⅛" x ¹⁄₁₆" on the top and bottom of the sheeting. An alternative method would be to cut the fullsize tailplane or fin ribs and then use a ½" x ¼" leading edge with perhaps ¼" x ¾" trailing edge to the tailplane. The ribs can then be stuck directly between the leading and trailing edges. To form the tip shape you could use a piece of ⅛" balsa sheet which is glued in on the centre line of the tailplane to form the tip shape. If this was to be used on a fabric covered tailplane then the leading edge would be fairly susceptible to damage or a sub leading edge would require letting in behind it. If this tailplane was being built for an all-sheet aircraft then to cover the structure with light ¹⁄₁₆" sheet top and bottom would result in a very rigid construction. Fig.49 gives the internal design for this type of tailplane or fin.

Elevators and rudders can be made using the same system but the material sizes would obviously require adapting to suit.

Before the tailplane, fin, rudder, elevator etc. are covered you will also need to glue in some pieces of half inch square balsa approximately 1" long which can be used to take the hinge points which are used to move the control surfaces.

The author's Miles Gemini twin not only has a pair of motors but also twin fins and rudders which require fitting to the ends of the tailplane.

Chapter 8

Concealed Control Surfaces

Concealed control surfaces or flush fitting ones are very much a feature of the later or faster flying aircraft. On a typical WW1 bi-plane, the trailing edge of the tailplane or fin would usually be square with the leading edge of the elevator or rudder equally square with a hinge mounted between. Quite often the resulting gap would be covered with a piece of fabric to stop the air blowing through the control surface and losing some of its effect. This method of hinging a control surface is still used today on some of the light homebuilt aircraft and is perfectly adequate at the speeds they fly at.

With the improvements in aircraft design and the speeds these aircraft were obtaining, greater streamlining was required and the gap between the control surfaces was obviously an area that needed improving. The flush fitting control surface is very common on the WW2 fighters for instance but there are many other light aircraft of the faster or later types which also feature this design innovation. If you are trying to make a half reasonable representation of your particular prototype and it features this type of control surface then it is well worth the effort of incorporating this type of hinging. You will also find an improvement in the flying qualities of the aircraft with crisper response from the elevator and rudder if you use the correct hinging and streamlining of the joint as opposed to having a gap between the control surfaces.

The basic method of constructing the tailplane will follow your normal methods but the rear spar is best made from at least quarter sheet balsa because the balsa sheeting to the top and bottom will be allowed to carry on past the rear spar of the tailplane. The elevator will be built along normal lines but the front of it will be faced with preferably quarter sheet balsa so that you can round the top and bottom edge of it. If the centre line of the hinge is going to be fairly close to the leading edge of the elevator then you may wish to use hinges such as the Robart hinge points. If you feel that there is too much unsupported hinge protruding from the rear of the tailplane you may wish to epoxy the hinge points into a brass tube which can then be epoxied into the rear of the tailplane. It is also a good idea if you cut pieces of ½" square balsa about 1" long and stick that to the inside of the tailplane rear spar so that there is plenty of wood for the hinge points to be stuck to. Similar balsa blocks can be fitted inside the elevator before the top sheeting is applied.

If on the other hand the hinge centre line is going to be some distance in from the leading edge of the tailplane as is depicted in Fig.50, it is best if the hinges are made from Tufnol. Tufnol is available in sheets of various sizes depending on your supplier and is a brown laminated material which is made from layers of cloth. A cheaper alternative which looks much the same is Paxolin but this is a paper laminate and does not have the same strength as Tufnol. Sheets of either material are available in various thicknesses but about 1⁄16" would be more than adequate for the majority of our applications – 3⁄32" x 1⁄8" on even third scale models should be alright.

Using this method of hinging, the elevator is built in two halves with pieces of ½" x 1" block built into the top and bottom halves of the elevator. If these blocks have a groove worked into them, pieces of brass tube can be epoxied into the groove in the centre line so that a 16swg piano wire pin the full span of the elevator can be slid in from a small hole in the tip enabling the tailplane and elevator to be assembled after the aircraft

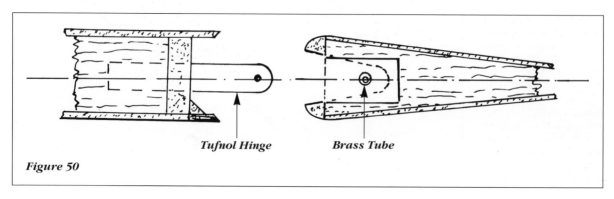

Tufnol Hinge   **Brass Tube**

Figure 50

The Japanese Zero modelled by Len Gardiner illustrates clearly the flush fitting control surfaces to the rudder and elevator along with frieze type ailerons.

has been painted etc. Of course the piano wire hinge can be slid in and out a number of times during assembly to check the fit of everything which would also enable you to cover and paint the aircraft with the control surfaces removed which could have definite advantages. Fig.51 gives you an idea of this method of construction and depicts the tailplane fully built whilst the elevator only has the bottom half drawn with the brass tubes in place and the piano wire waiting to be slid in when everything is lined up correctly. If you are building a particularly large model which is going to be difficult to transport in your car and you wished to remove the rudder or elevator for transportation purposes, this could be a good way of doing it. You will need to bend over the end of the piano wire so that it can be pulled out for removal but with a little imagination anything should be possible! In Fig.50 the top and bottom sheeting to the tailplane pro-

trudes beyond the rear spar and is unsupported which would be alright on a smaller model but might be fragile on a somewhat larger aircraft. The alternative to this would be to make the overhanging portion with the grain in the opposite direction and supported on a small triangular bead glued into the top and bottom corners.

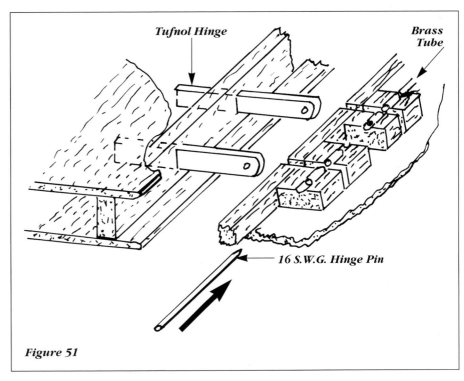

Tufnol Hinge

Brass Tube

16 S.W.G. Hinge Pin

Figure 51

Chapter 9

Building Wing Fillets

Take a look at virtually any of the WW2 fighters and you will realise that they have at least two things in common. Firstly they are low wing monoplane aircraft and secondly they have wing fillets blending the wing into the side of the fuselage. With aircraft flying at higher speeds, improvements in aerodynamics were needed to realise the performance that the more powerful engines provided. In aerodynamic terms there can be quite a bit of drag caused where the wing meets the fuselage so to help smooth this out wing fillets will produce quite a dramatic improvement in this area of an aircraft.

Another feature of fullsize aircraft design is that in most cases their wings are not built as a one piece unit which we modellers tend to make as the norm! In a lot of cases the wing spars are built into the fuselage and terminate at very substantial fixing points on the edge of the fuselage. The wings have the spars terminating with matching fixings which are bolted onto the side of the fuselage. This results in a gap between the fuselage and wing and the fairing is used to cover this gap up. One of the advantages fullsize pilots have over modellers is that when they have finished flying their aircraft for the day they just wheel it into a hangar rather than having to take the wings off it! By leaving their aircraft fully assembled, the wing fillets can be secured to the side of the fuselage and wing which holds them firmly in place. We, on the other hand, can build the wing fillets to the side of the fuselage but they cannot be attached permanently to the wing for obvious reasons. The great problem here is that when the thin edge of the wing fillet makes contact with the wing it invariably wants to curl and lift away from the wing surface leaving an unsightly gap. I must admit that over the years I have built quite a few wing fillets but I do find it to be one of the less enjoyable aspects of building a scale model!

There are many different forms of wing fillets but we will look at the basic construction. When the model is being designed you will need to decide whether the leading edge of the wing carries right the way through the fuselage or whether it is stepped back to the main spar. This can give you quite a few advantages depending on the particular type of fillets applied to the aircraft. Some aircraft may have very little in the way of

Wing Cut Back To Spars

Figure 52

The author's Avro Anson features very large and distinctive wing fillets.

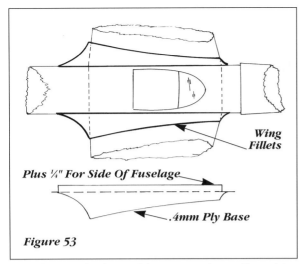

Plus ¼" For Side Of Fuselage

Wing Fillets

.4mm Ply Base

Figure 53

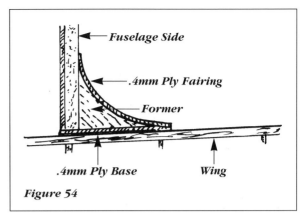

Fuselage Side

.4mm Ply Fairing

Former

.4mm Ply Base   Wing

Figure 54

wing fillet on the front of the wing and virtually nothing below it. See Fig.52 for details of the two basic wing types.

The best method I have found to make wing fillets is to start by cutting .4mm ply to the plan shape of the wing fillets allowing sufficient to go under the wing seat and be glued to the fuselage sides. Fig.53 illustrates the shape the ply would be cut to. When you are cutting the wing seat for the aircraft allow the additional .4mm to accept this ply whilst keeping the wing in its correct

position. When you glue the .4mm ply in place you will need to bolt the wing in its correct position to hold the ply whilst the glue dries. You can then pin the various formers on with a spacing of two or three inches. These formers should start at the main spar position and go back to the trailing edge of the wing. See Fig.54.

This portion of the wing fillet can now be completed using .4mm ply with the grain running in the long direction. Cut your piece of ply a little oversize and bend it into position and see how it fits. It may take quite a bit of adjusting to get this piece to fit exactly but when you are satisfied you can glue it in place. If the wing fillet has too many curves in it then it would not be possible

The underview of the Avro Anson with the wing removed to show construction of the wing fillets. Note that the wing leading edge has been taken back to the main spar to go through the fuselage. This was done to make the forward portion of wing fillets easier to build to the fuselage.

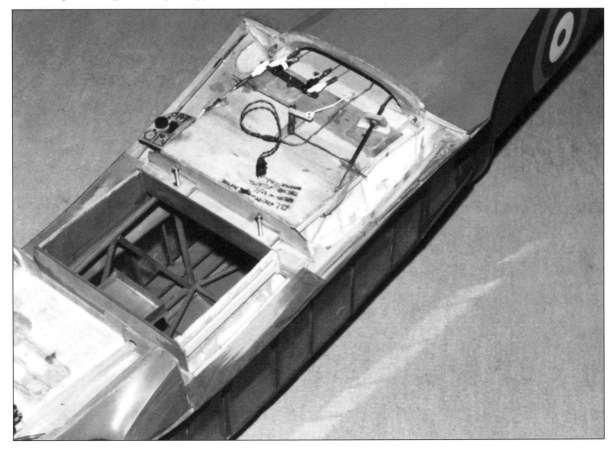

The wing fillets around the engine nacelle are small enough to build up using lightweight filler.

shrinking agent, it will invariably cause the wing fillet to lift away from the wing. Nothing looks worse than the tell-tale gap that demonstrates quite blatantly that your wing fillets are not screwed to the wing which is what you are trying to simulate! If you are trying to simulate a thin sheet of metal as a wing fillet you will also need to have a fairly fine edge to your fillet if it is going to look at all realistic. These two requirements are obviously potential problem areas so a method I have seen used on quite a few occasions is to actually build up the wing so that the wing fillet can drop into the recess, thereby concealing the joint between the wing fillet and the wing. Fig.55 illustrates this.

to form the main part using .4mm ply. The alternative would be to plank in with balsa by cutting strips of ⅛" sheet around ¾" wide. As the fillet from the main spar to the leading edge is usually highly curved this can either be carved from solid light balsa and then glued in place or alternatively, if the fillet is fairly small, it would be quite acceptable to use one of the very lightweight fillers mixed with polyester or epoxy resin.

In most cases the fillet is carried on beyond the trailing edge of the wing and is usually flat or lightly curved on the underside. If the piece of quarter balsa sheet is cut to the required shape it can be glued to the side of the fuselage and to the bottom piece of .4mm ply. You do need to be careful not to stick this to the wing. Depending on the shape of the wing fillets it might be possible to extend the curved top piece of ply over this or, alternatively, you may need to build up some laminations of quarter balsa sheet and sand to shape.

When you have your perfectly shaped fillet which is bedded down nicely on top of the wing, you might think the job is now completely sorted out . . . and you may now be approaching the downfall of the entire project! If when you come to cover the fillet you proceed to use dope and tissue, you will find that since dope is a

If the additional sheeting which is applied to the top of the wing is blended in over three or four inches of the span, it should be nearly impossible to detect that this is the method you have used to enable you to produce a thicker edge to your wing fillets without detracting from scale appearance. As already mentioned, covering with dope and tissue can generate problems that we do not want. A far better system is the glass skinning method using epoxy resin. This method of covering contributes a lot to the strength of the fillet and of course since epoxy resin is not a shrinking agent it will not induce any warping tendencies into the fairing. It would be a good idea to brush some resin into the underside of the fairing to give it a little extra strength as well although fully glass-skinning this area would probably result in the wing no longer fitting the cut-out properly.

On some twin-engined aircraft you quite often find that the engine nacelles have small fillets blending them into the wings. These are sufficiently small to be built up using lightweight filler. Fillers such as microballoons which is a K.&.B. product would be ideally suited for this purpose. There are also even lighter fillers available which are generally sold for making fillets with. In both cases they can be mixed with normal polyester glassfibre resins or epoxy wing skinning resins. When these fillers have set they can then be sanded to the correct profile quite easily ready for covering at a later stage.

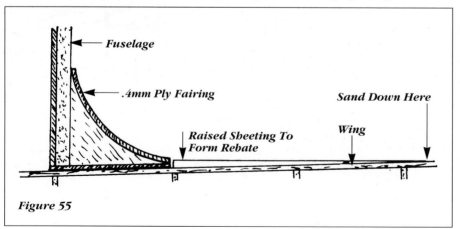

Figure 55

Chapter 10

Installing Servos within a Scale Model

You may be wondering what is so special about installing the radio gear in a scale model. If by now you have built one or two sport models you will have certainly fitted the radio successfully but it would be fair to say that a sport model is designed to be functional and if some of the linkages are visible on the outside then they are there for a reason – it is also far more practical to do it that way. In a sports model, you will have a large compartment when the wing is removed from the fuselage in which you can easily install the radio gear. The aircraft will also have been designed to achieve the correct centre of gravity without too much careful repositioning of the radio! With a scale model we have the shape already designed for us so we have to fit our model requirements within this given shape and as we have to achieve the correct centre of gravity it is far nicer if this can be done without adding lumps of lead into the nose of the aircraft.

It is well worth trying to position all the radio gear as far forward as possible to try and help in this requirement. Obviously to bury a NiCad in the front of an aircraft presents no particular problems. All one has to do is route the lead from it to the switch and on to the receiver which should not present too many problems. On the other hand the servos need a linkage connected and then routed to the appropriate control surface. On smaller models of around 72" wing span or less it is perfectly practical to have a centrally mounted servo in the wing driving 16swg pushrods working via bellcranks. The linkage from the bellcrank will exit the wing surface at the appropriate scale point to drive the ailerons. If it is a concealed control surface the linkage will need to be kept within the wing to operate the aileron. As aircraft have progressively got bigger – quarter scale bi-planes are commonplace now

– and with the wings being detachable in separate panels from the fuselage, alternative systems have been devised. True, it would still be perfectly practical to use a centrally mounted servo but then some method of connecting the 16swg wire with quicklinks to the servo would need to be found. This is not a very practical solution and what is far better is to use a pair of aileron servos.

There are many advantages to this system. Firstly a pair of servos will produce twice the power of a single one which would be beneficial with the larger models requiring more power to operate the larger control surfaces. Secondly, if you have a pair of aileron servos, in the event of one failing in flight the other would carry on working and enable you to get the aircraft back down on the ground safely. Thirdly by having the aileron servo mounted directly in line with the aileron, the linkage can be kept much shorter and a far more positive connection made.

The aileron servo lead will need extending and a plug will then hang out of the wing rib which butts the fuselage side. A socket can be built into the fuselage side at the appropriate place and connected to the receiver. When you assemble the model all you then need to do is to plug in the aileron lead to the fuselage

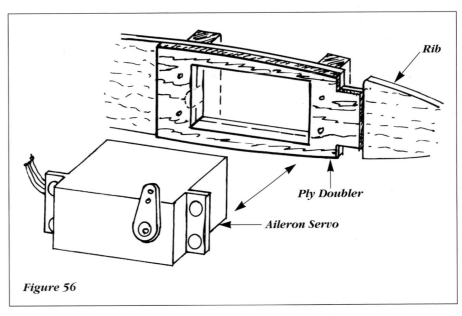

Rib

Ply Doubler

Aileron Servo

Figure 56

The micro Multiplex servo fitted directly to the wing rib with a ply doubler attached.

side and continue assembling the model. With my quarter scale SE5A, Tiger Moth and Hanriot HD-1 the wing ribs are just sufficiently deep to fit standard ballrace servos on their side. See Fig.56. There are also some good quality micro servos on the market which would enable you to fit individual servos in even thinner wings with the advantage of a direct control linkage. In most cases the wing ribs would be made from 3/32" sheet balsa and there is no way that you could directly fix the servo to that so before the wing ribs are built into the wing it is a simple matter to stick a piece of 1/16" ply onto the side of the rib in the appropriate position. The position of the servo will usually be determined by any external linkage that is connected to the aileron horns and you will need to decide where the servo has to be to connect directly to that. If on the other hand you are fitting the servos into a wing that has a concealed linkage such as my Beech 18 then I have positioned the servos as far forward as is possible to help with the centre of gravity.

The piece of ply should also be taken over the section of wing rib that has the spar cut-outs in it. The piece of ply can be stuck to the wing rib and left a little oversize and then cut and sanded to the correct shape when the glue has dried. The spar cut-outs will also need cutting in. Place the servo onto the ply portion of the rib in its correct position and mark around it. To cut out the rectangle, drill out the corners and then with a coping saw or fret saw it should be fairly easy to remove the centre piece. If you do not have either of these types of saw then a fairly stout blade in a scalpel should make the necessary cuts for you to remove the ply and balsa that way. Check the fit of the servo and file out any portion of the cut-out that is not giving you sufficient clearance.

If the lead comes out of the servo below the mounting lug you will need to file a notch in the end of the cut-out to allow that to pass through. It is also a good idea to cut some pieces of quarter ply about 3/8" wide x

3/4" long which can be glued to the balsa side of the cut-out. The advantage of these blocks is that when you screw the servo in place through the 1/16" ply the screw tips will go through into the quarter ply on the other side and hold the servos securely in place. It is worth remembering of course that once the wing is covered then gaining access to the servos will be very difficult indeed. If you feel that access is important and you are not too worried about scale appearance then some form of hatch could be built into the bottom wing covering.

One advantage of going for a true scale appearance on a fabric covered wing is that the wing ribs have pinking tapes over them. If I wished to gain access to my aileron servo then I would have to be bold and cut-out the covering using a sharp scalpel to get at it. When the necessary work had been done I could then re-cover the appropriate bay or bays and conceal the fact that I had cut the covering by fitting new pinking tapes over the tops of the ribs and covering the joint.

It may seem an obvious remark but if you are going to bury the servos perhaps using a better quality of servo rather than the cheapest one you can find would be a good idea at this point. I like to use a double ballrace servo in these areas as well. Another advantage with using individual aileron servos is that if you are using one of the modern computer radios, you can drive the servos from two different channels. If your transmitter can electronically mix the two channels to work as one then you will have individual adjustments for the top, bottom and middle travel points of both servos. With a total of six adjustments available for your servos you should be able to set it up to cover most situations. This method of fixing servos for flaps would be equally practical.

When it comes to mounting the servos in the fuselage you should have a much greater degree of accessibility to them in the event of them requiring maintenance. The main problem with the fuselage is that although the cockpit area would be an ideal place for fitting the servos, if you wish to keep it clear to maintain true scale appearance you simply have to find somewhere else! Elevator and rudder servos may be mounted on their side under the pilot's seat which should be made removable for access if required. The method of fixing the servos in place would be to cut a sheet of 1/8" ply the required size and proceed to make the servo cut-outs within this plate. You may be able to make a plate which would take two or three servos and conceal them quite successfully. Alternatively, you may wish to make

Scale Construction

one plate to take a servo and mount another one in a different place altogether. I have, on several models, managed to get the elevator and rudder servo right up into the nose or even in the engine compartment of an aircraft. I have then connected a tube and cable to either take it through the cockpit area or bury it under the floor. When the tube and cable has passed the cockpit area it can then be attached to a ½" x ¼" balsa pushrod and taken

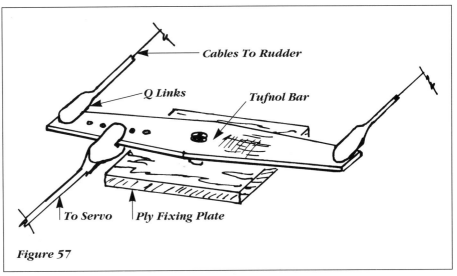

Figure 57

directly to the elevator linkage. Another method that could be used here is to connect the tube and cable to a cross bar and then use a closed loop system for rudder, elevator etc operated from that. See Fig.57.

The throttle servo will be mounted in the front of the aircraft so that it can be connected directly to the carburettor. I have in fact mounted throttle servos in the engine compartment itself on several models although I have no doubt that the radio manufacturers would totally disapprove of me doing this and strongly advise against it. Obviously vibration levels in the engine compartment are the highest to be found in any model and has the potential to shake the servo to pieces. Certainly I would only use good quality ballrace servos in this installation. At the same time I would only suggest doing it if you are determined to keep the model as light as you can or to keep it within some imposed competition weight limits.

It is worth remembering that competition weight limits have little – if anything – to do with safety factors. It would certainly be good advice to keep the servos as far forward as you can whilst nevertheless keeping them behind the firewall. This will also stop them getting covered in fuel and oil. Some of the better quality servos have fine rubber "O" rings between the various parts of the case with the intention of keeping water out of them in boat use.

These "O" rings will also keep fuel and oil out of our aircraft servos. I have also found with experience that fuel and oil follows the laws of gravity very successfully so providing your servos are mounted above the engine and away from any splashing caused by the carburettor they should remain comparatively clean.

Twin Elevator Servos

I have already mentioned the advantages of using a pair of aileron servos inasmuch as they double the power available and increase the reliability in the event of a servo failing. The elevator, however, is arguably the most important control on the aircraft especially if you are in a steep dive and need to recover! As the dive establishes itself, there will be an obvious build up of speed and the forces required to move the elevator will greatly increase with the speed. Larger models have larger control surfaces and these certainly require more power to move them. Whilst there are plenty of large or 'quarter scale' servos as they are called that will generate that extra power, you may prefer to use a pair of standard type servos working together as a means of operating the elevator. The obvious advantage is that you still get twice the power but in the event of one of them failing, at least you have half your normal control over this important function. The basic installation is illustrated in Fig.58. This comprises the two servos mounted side by side with a cross bar connected to the output discs. The connections to the discs will need to be on the same

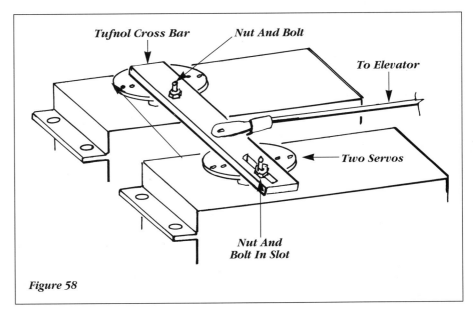

Figure 58

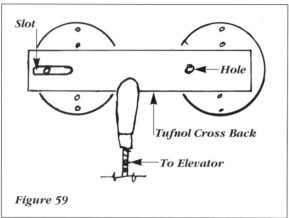

Figure 59

a good idea to use metal in this application as it would be an unnecessary source of metal to metal joints which could possibly cause radio interference.

With the increased power from a pair of elevator servos it is also worth considering your elevator linkage and whether it is of sufficient strength. Certainly with a single servo, using ½" x ¼" balsa with a middle support along the fuselage would be quite adequate. With a pair of servos half inch square with maybe two supports would be a good idea. To eliminate slop and poor response your control linkage should be kept as straight as possible in order to avoid unnecessary kinks or bends in it.

side of each servo. The elevator pushrod will then be connected to the middle of this cross bar. With both servos working in the same direction and with the same amount of travel you will experience no problems at all. If one servo stops or the servos do not have equal movement then the system will bind up solid. The simple answer to this problem is to cut a slot in the cross bar to allow for one of the servos moving to its full travel without the other moving at all. Fig.59 illustrates this.

The cross bar for the servos should be made from material such as Tufnol but Paxolin will suffice if you cannot get hold of the former. Certainly it would not be

With an aircraft such as the quarter scale Sirocco, when the wing is removed good access can be gained to the fuselage so that the servos, receiver and NiCad can be mounted as far forward as possible.

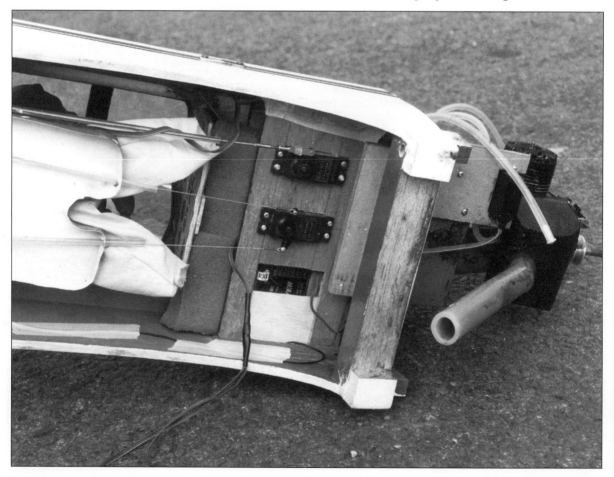

Chapter 11

Closed Loop Control Systems

O n a number of early fullsize aircraft the control surfaces were operated via cables and wires. Numerous WW1 bi-planes had all the flying controls operated this way and the wires were routed along the outside of the aircraft with most of the control runs very visible indeed. Later aircraft like the Tiger Moth had the rudder and elevator operated this way whilst the Avro Anson for instance had only the ailerons operated by this method. So should we as modellers copy fullsize and go for a closed loop system or should we go for internal pushrods which, in a lot of models, would be very hard to conceal indeed? If you only intend to put a large plastic commercial horn on the control surface and connect it with a quicklink and pushrod then it is not going to do a lot for the looks of your new scale model!

I have used closed loop on many of my scale models over the years with a great deal of success. I will be the first to admit that when I decided to try and use a closed loop system I was very tentative about it. I felt at the time that the rudder was probably the least important control on the model so if the system was going to give me problems it wouldn't be too drastic. Nowadays I regard a closed loop system as almost standard practice for connecting the rudder, in particular, since two lengths of control line Laystrate are considerably lighter than any pushrod and quicklinks that I would be happy to use.

The two types of Laystrate wire which I regularly use are the lightweight ones made from three strands of steel wire soldered together which means it is pre-tinned and the heavyweight made from seven strands of steel wire soldered together. The lighter Laystrate wire is of little use except perhaps on very small scale models.

The author's 1/4 scale Sirocco which has a closed loop control system for the rudder.

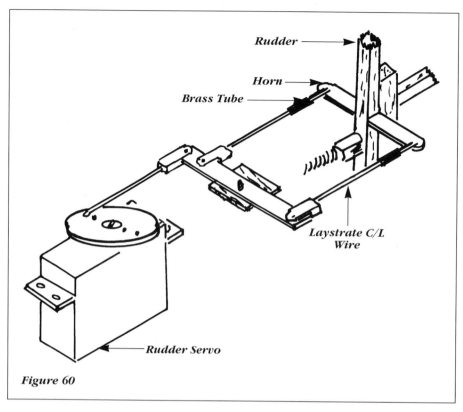

Rudder

Horn

Brass Tube

Laystrate C/L Wire

Rudder Servo

Figure 60

Alternatives to Laystrate wire are the various forms of nylon covered steel wires which are made for fishing lines and would be available from any fishing supply shop. Using this system where the control horns would be completely scale in appearance. I have found this very convenient where the rudder horn is mounted within the model and therefore is totally enclosed – here you are looking for 100% reliability! I have also found it useful for connecting the linkage to a steerable tailwheel which almost invariably has an enclosed linkage which has to be completely reliable to withstand the abuse that a tailwheel can be subjected to. Fig.60 depicts a

Peter McDermott's DH9A exudes a wealth of scale detail. Note the working closed loop wires for the rudder and elevator which protrude through the fuselage side.

typical closed loop system used for operating the rudder where part of the linkage will be on the outside of the aircraft. This will come in through the side of the fuselage at the appropriate scale point and small lengths of plastic tube should be used to guide it through the fuselage sides to act as bearings.

The rudder horn should ideally be made from Tufnol. It needs to be cut to scale size and shape as closely as possible in order to produce the scale effect that we are looking for although if the horn can be kept an inch each side of the control surface that should be regarded as a practical minimum if the scale requirements permit this to be done.

When you are attaching the Laystrate wire to the horn it is best if a small piece of brass tube approximately ¼" to ⅜" long is slid over both lengths of wire which will then make it very easy indeed to soft solder everything in place and retain the wires. This will also have the advantage of looking as if you have fitted scale adjusters into the closed loop system and the appearance can be further enhanced with appropriate paint at a later stage.

It would seem logical at first to connect your two Laystrate control line wires directly to the output disc or bar of the servo, but there are two good reasons for NOT doing this. Firstly as the wires are under light tension all the time this will put a sideways load onto the output shaft of the servo which in turn will cause rather higher wear than is acceptable on the servo. If space does not permit then you can connect directly to the servo but at least try and make sure that the servo is a reasonable size and quality and has a ballbearing – or preferably two ballraces – on the output shaft to give the servo a slight chance in life! What is far better is to con-

nect your two Laystrate wires to an idler bar which can be fixed to a suitable ply plate somewhere in the fuselage. Quicklinks can be fitted to the end of the Laystrate wire which in turn are connected to the idler bar but these quicklinks will be used purely to tension the system and take up any slack which may be produced over the years. To connect the idler bar to the servo you can use a normal quicklink and rod and this will have the advantage that if you need to adjust the control surface to produce a little right or left trim etc. you only have to adjust one quicklink from the servo to produce the desired deflection.

On some scale models the scale size horn will be far smaller than you would ideally choose so if you connect into the outer hole in the wheel of your output disc you will have far more deflection on your rudder than you would actually require. So if the idler bar is made somewhat longer on one side than is needed to connect the Laystrate wires to, this can be used as a very convenient method of gearing down the movement whist still maintaining a good mechanical linkage which will be free of slop. If the idler bar can also be mounted somewhere in the fuselage where you can gain access to it then you would be able to adjust the amount of rudder or control surface movement at a later stage when you have found what you actually require after having flown the model a few times.

On my Avro Anson the aileron horns protrude about 1" above and below the aileron which is an ideal situation on a model but as the ailerons are fairly small on this particular aircraft they require quite a large deflection. I didn't need to get rid of any movement that the servo could produce so I connected directly to the

Your author's SE5A flying back from a dawn patrol raid over the opposition territory. This aircraft of course features a closed loop system to operate the rudder which has large horns conveniently for us modellers.

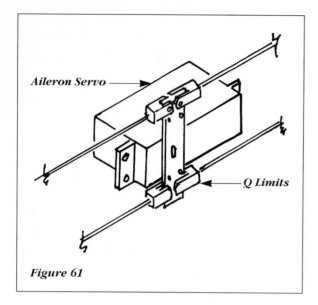

Figure 61

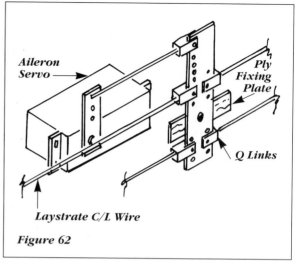

Figure 62

aileron servo as depicted in Fig.61. Although at first appearance you could say I was abusing the servo, in fact when you think about it the closed loop system is pulling directly through the output disc onto the closed loop system of the other side rather than directly onto the servo itself as it would do in the case of the rudder servo. The servo which I used in this particular case had twin ballraces to the output shaft and lasted several years with no problems.

The first aircraft I made using Laystrate control wires to operate the ailerons was my 57" span Sirocco. The horns on this particular aircraft were a lot smaller and I needed to get rid of some of the movement that the aileron servo was producing. Fig.62 shows the way I reduced this movement using an idler bar but, if you think about it, it is basically an adaptation of Fig.60 and 61. In Fig.62 four closed loop quicklinks are used only to tension the system whereas the quicklink on the

pushrod going through to the servo will be used to determine the amount of movement depending where it is positioned on the idler bar and of course will be the only quicklink which would need adjusting to produce a little bit of left or right hand trim, which you may wish to incorporate in the model as you find necessary.

On WW1 bi-planes the ailerons were operated by a closed loop system in the following manner. The control cable was routed through the bottom wing, round a small pulley (in model terms this works out at ¼" to ½" diameter) then out via the bottom covering of the wing to the aileron horn on the bottom aileron. It carries on to the top aileron via a stout wire or pushrod and then is connected from the top aileron horn around another small pulley across the top wing and repeats the process on the other side to form a complete circuit. Various modellers who have tried to duplicate this system say that the size of the pulleys and stiffness or relative stiffness of the wire does not really work in practice however powerful a servo you have in the fuselage to drive it.

This Albatros aircraft would be typical of the period when all the controls were operated closed loop and with many of the cables being visible.

The practical solution nowadays is to use a pair of aileron servos and to make a dummy closed loop system. This has all the advantages of powerful servos on a short direct linkage with good aileron response. Producing a scale looking aileron linkage will complete the illusion that you are trying to create.

Chapter 12

Tool Kits

When you look through magazines such as R/C Model World these days, it would be easy to get the impression that you really don't have to do very much building at all. Reading the advertisement hype such as "almost ready to fly" "quick assembly" "laser cut this, CNC cut that" indicates that there is virtually no building to do. The general idea seems to be that when you have purchased your kit and brought it home all you need to do is to open the lid of the box, squirt in some glue, shake for 5 minutes and out would pop a completely ready to fly aircraft!

Many of the kits these days do have parts cut out for you very accurately indeed and there is not a lot more to do than basic assembly. There are other modellers, however, who much prefer to buy a scale plan with perhaps a glassfibre cowl and canopy and cut all their own wood

knowing that at the end of the day they have actually created the model that they wish to fly.

Even with the better almost-ready-to-fly models I suspect there is still a certain amount of building to do – at the very least you will have to fit your radio, engine, fuel tank etc. into the model which will require some woodworking along with the necessary tools to do the job. If you are scratch building from a plan or if you design the aircraft yourself you are going to need a reasonable selection of tools.

One of the things I have noticed over the years is that quite a number of modellers are more than happy to spend large amounts of money on chrome covered radios and engines with whistles and bells all over the place. These are fitted in an aircraft, flown and nobody seem too worried if they get crashed – it's just one of

The most used modelling tool of all is a decent quality knife for cutting balsa and thin ply. Illustrated are three types of Swan Morton scalpels which will accept quite a wide variety of blades. Handle types shown are 3, 4 and 5. Replacement blades come wrapped in metal foil are quickly refitted in the handles. The Stanley knife can be very useful for cutting 1/16" ply or even thicker if you do not have an appropriate saw for the job.

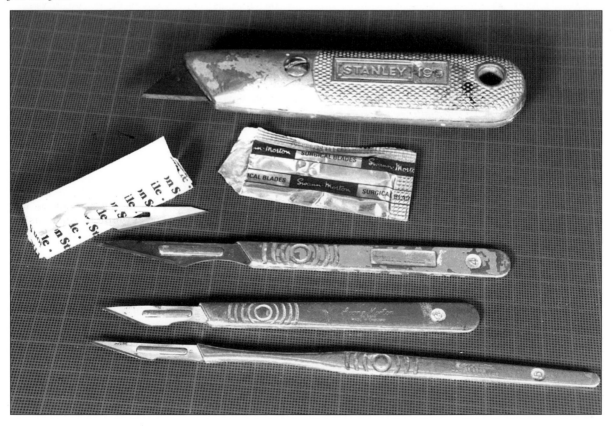

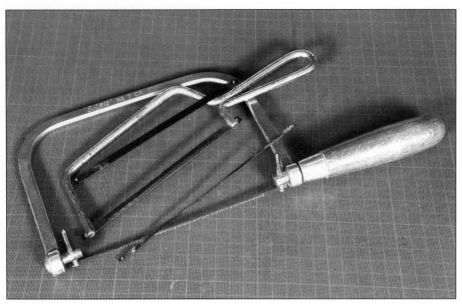

Two types of saws which would be invaluable for modelling work. The larger one is a coping saw and has the feature that the blade can be rotated through a full 360° and is easily removable from the frame. The smaller one is a junior backsaw which is meant for cutting metal but will also cut glassfibre and wood equally well with its fine teeth.

those things! Suggest that they buy some decent quality tools so that they could build the model more easily and they are very reluctant to spend the money.

One thing is for sure – tools are never going to get crashed at the flying site and wise investment should last you your entire modelling life. I served my apprenticeship as a carpenter and joiner many years ago and am still using a lot of the tools I bought on my apprentice wages.

The most used tool of all when making balsa aircraft (or even when using the thinner grades of ply) is a decent quality knife. It is surprising how many modellers

Two types of sandpaper blocks which are commercially available. The one in the foreground is made from cork whilst top right corner is solid rubber. This is ideal for using with wet-and-dry paper when used wet. The large block of melamine is a homemade sandpaper block. Also illustrated is a small David plane useful for rough shaping and a good quality putty knife for mixing up fillers.

use poor quality knives and wonder why the job is difficult. I have used quite a number of different types over the years and currently am using the Swan Morton scalpels. There are a selection of handles which take different types of blades and these clip into the handles which holds them very firmly. The great advantage is that if a blade is beginning to get blunt you just take it out and put in a new one. The handles I use are nos. 3, 4 and 5. The no. 3 handle takes a 10A blade, no. 4 has a 26 blade and is very useful for cutting the larger pieces of wood. The no. 5 handle will take a no. 11 blade which is very suitable for fine, delicate cutting out work and is my favourite blade when it comes to masking a model up ready for painting or cutting out stencils as you have very fine control with it. The handles are not particularly expensive and the blades are purchased in packs of five. Most of the handles will take two or three different styles of blade making them versatile. The knives should be obtainable from the better model shops or any of the graphic art supply shops.

The Stanley knife might be regarded as rather a heavyweight knife and not suitable for cutting balsa but in fact it is ideal for cutting out 1/16" ply as you can really put pressure on it. Also with this knife there are replacement blades available and there are several styles of blade although I find the straight one to be the most useful.

When you are cutting components that require a straight line you do need some form of steel straight edge. There are many steel rulers one foot long (or should I say 300mm these days) which are ideal for our modelling purposes. It is best if you buy one that has imperial and metric measurements on it. There are also aluminium rulers around which are at least 1m long and usually have imperial and metric measurements on them which make them ideal for cutting a full sheet of balsa down its length. Whilst talking of rulers the steel tapes that retract within the small box can also be very useful for measuring wing spans, lengths of fuselages etc. Again buying a metric/imperial one would be the sensible way to go these days.

Whilst talking metric/imperial I notice that if you buy a sheet of plywood it is quoted in a metric measurement and the figures are not that logical. The reason is very simple, however, when you put an imperial ruler on it – the sheets always were and still are exactly 8ft. x 4ft. So much for metrication!

The knives I have suggested will certainly cut up to 1/16" ply and maybe 3/16" or even 1/4" balsa by taking several cuts at it but obviously things like ¼" ply will not cut with a knife. For cutting such parts as fuselage formers out of ⅛" or ¼" ply a coping saw is almost invaluable. With this saw it is very easy to cut round curves or other irregular shape. Its other useful feature is that the blade can be rotated around a full 360°, enabling many otherwise awkward pieces to be cut-out easily. If for instance you had a bandsaw, cutting out a fuselage former would be easy but if you wished to cut the centre of the former out this is completely impossible with the continuous blade that is used on a bandsaw. This is where the coping saw comes into its own since, if you drill a ¼" hole through the middle of the former, the blade from the coping saw can be passed through that and then the saw reassembled. When this has been done it is easy to cut out the middle of the former. Dismantle the saw and the job is complete.

The example I have been using for many years was manufactured by Eclipse and is well worth the small cost.

Still on the subject of saws the junior hacksaw is also a very useful tool. Although primarily designed for cutting metal with its fine toothed blades, it is equally suitable for cutting wood. Trying to cut a piece of ½" thick balsa with a knife, particularly across the grain, is not an easy job but a junior hacksaw will cut across very easily. Replacement blades can be fitted when the teeth start to get worn just as they can with the coping saw previously mentioned. One of the little tricks that you can use the junior hacksaw blades for is that if you remove the retaining pins from the end it can be used as a slot cutter. If you wish to cut slots for flat plate hinges the end of the blade can be pushed into the wood and then pulled backwards and forwards to form a slot ready for hinging your model. I have found many uses for this technique other than fitting hinges over the years. Of course a junior hacksaw will not just work on wood and metal but is also very well suited for cutting glassfibre with its fine teeth.

With some aircraft, the designer will have suggested that you glue a large lump of wood in position then carve it to shape, particularly for wing tips etc. Some of the large pieces you may be able to carve away with a scalpel but a small plane would be very useful for this job. There is one such available which is called a David plane and is fitted with a razor blade as a cutter. This can be very suitable for getting a

piece of wood to roughly the right shape in preparation for sanding.

One of the biggest areas that make a model either poorly finished or superbly produced is the amount of sanding that the modeller has done to produce a good surface in preparation for covering and painting. There are many sandpaper blocks on the market and the ones with the cork backing are ideal for general wood sanding. I have also got a hard solid rubber one which is very useful for using with wet-and-dry paper at the painting and finishing stage of the model. The rest of the sandpaper blocks I have lying around my workbench were never bought at all as they off-cuts of wood of all sorts of shapes and sizes which have been used for specific purposes. For instance if you wish to rub down the top of a set of wing ribs to make sure that they all line up, the larger the sand paper block the better because then it will only remove the high spots which is what you want to get rid of and will level everything up. I have found off-cuts of melamine (the white plastic covered chipboard used in kitchen units, shelves etc.) can be very useful for this purpose. Whilst on the subject of sanding the old type glasspapers have been vastly improved by the introduction of the more modern "production" papers which are used in industry these days. There are a number of these production papers available from tool suppliers or D-I-Y superstores and they are well worth the slightly higher cost. For general sanding of balsa a medium paper is more than adequate and then you should go to a finer grade paper for finishing work. It is also a good idea not to carry on using a piece of paper once it has lost its cutting edge as it will be far

Two types of crosshead screwdriver are the Phillips on the left and Pozi on the right. The two outer screws are Pozi with the one in the middle being Phillips. Note the additional square within the cross of the Pozi screwdriver which is the distinguishing feature.

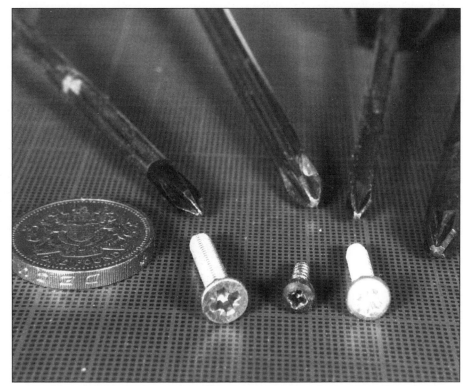

less effective and produce poor results. Using new paper will enable you to work with much lighter pressures and produce far better results.

Whilst sanding a model down there are likely to be dents in the wood which will need filling. The subject of fillers is beyond the scope of this book but a decent quality putty knife is ideal for mixing the fillers and then working them into the model. The example I have illustrated which has been in use for many a year is rather a nice one as it has an aluminium handle which enables me to clean all sorts of fillers from it with the appropriate thinners. This would be a problem with a putty knife with a wooden handle and its usual type of varnish finish.

When I was an apprentice you only needed two or three sizes of screwdriver and they would fit virtually every screw that you came across. In those days screws only had the simple slot head but now there are Phillips and Pozi to name the most popular crossheads but there are also others around as well. Needless to say a Pozi screwdriver will not work very well on a Phillips headed screw nor vice-versa. It is almost essential that you have the correct Phillips and pozi screwdrivers in their various sizes so that you have the appropriate one for whatever type of screw you are using. Also these days many of the bolts and self-tapping screws come with these type of heads. At a quick glance both are a cross head screwdriver although the pozi is the more complicated one as

it has further additional squares within the corners of the cross which distinguishes it from the Phillips which is just a simple cross. Also the length of the two screwdrivers is different which again makes them non-interchangeable. As you will be using screws or bolts to hold your engine, engine mount, undercarriage etc. in place, getting a selection of the medium to smaller sizes would be a good idea. Although I have just talked about the cross head screwdriver the straight slotted screw of yesteryear is still very much in vogue so two or three small to medium size screwdrivers would be an advantage.

If you are using nuts and bolts some form of spanner will be needed of the correct size. Modellers have traditionally used BA nuts and bolts but these days the metric variety are becoming very popular. With metric bolts if you measure the diameter which is say 3mm then that is known as an M3 bolt. Its length will be from the tip of the bolt to the underside of the head, so a typical example might be quoted as M3x25. For the appropriate nuts it is very easy to work out which spanner you require as you measure the width across the head and if it is 6mm you then need a 6mm socket or spanner to fit it.

There is a tool known as a box driver which looks very much like a screwdriver but has a hexagon socket on the end which will fit a nut. These are available in BA and metric sizes and can be useful for reaching down into an engine compartment for tightening up engine nuts and bolts etc. Open-ended spanners can

Three sizes of box driver for tightening nuts left. Also shown metric socket driver with interchangeable heads. Whilst right is a box spanner along with an open-ended spanner both of which are of the BA sizes.

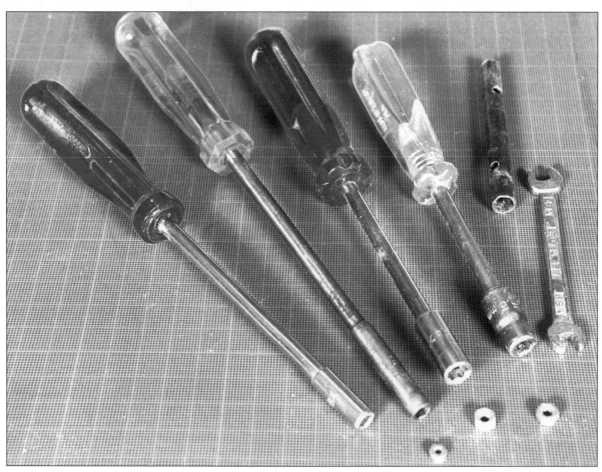

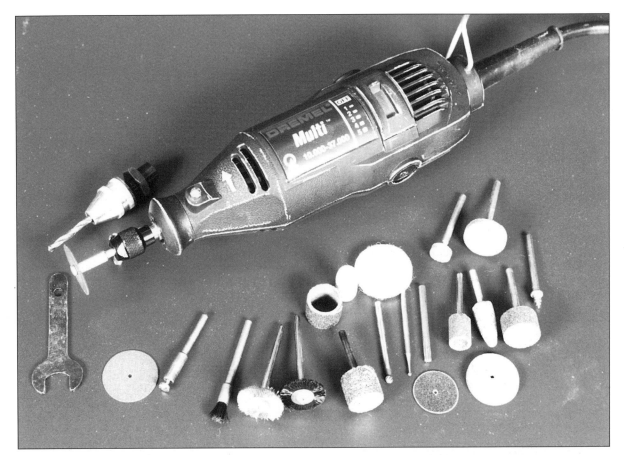

The mains powered Dremel drill has a speed range of 10 to 37000rpm. Illustrated are just a few of the accessories which include grinders, Cutting discs, polishers etc. The additional three-jaw chuck is very useful for accepting a wide range of drills.

also have their uses around an engine compartment. If you see some in either BA or metric sizes they would be well worth investing in.

One of the things that a kit manufacturer will most likely not have done for you is to drill holes in formers so that you can fit tubes and cables to work your control surfaces. There are many other situations where holes will need to be drilled and it is a very good idea to buy a set of metric drills which are readily available. Buying a set from perhaps 1.5 through to 6mm would cover most situations but instead of buying the sets which go in .5mm increments it is worth looking out for and paying the extra money for the sets which go in .1mm increments. You might feel that this is a little excessive but it is surprising how many of the odd sizes you need, particularly if you are drilling holes to fit piano wire which is not in metric sizes but old standard wire gauges – for instance a hole to suit 6swg wire is 4.9mm where a 5mm hole would be quite slack for it. These drill sets should be obtainable from any engineering supply stockists. Imperial or metric drill sets in .5mm increments would be readily obtainable from D-I-Y stores.

Having bought your drills you need something to work them in and here the choice is vast. There are, for example, the simple hand drills which must represent very good value indeed. Nowadays most modellers want to use electric examples and there are small and cheap 12v ones readily available. These usually feature collet chucks which will accept 2 or 3 sizes of drill to fit prop-

erly. These have the advantage of being small as already mentioned so if you have forgotten to drill a hole in the depths of the fuselage you can do this at a later stage quite easily.

Fairly recently I had the pleasure of reviewing one of the Dremel drills for Radio Control Model World magazine and was very impressed with the quality and performance of the tool. It is a little larger than the aforementioned 12v drills but as it works from the mains

The drill cutter which is fitted in the Dremel drill can be very useful for cutting out slots or air in-takes on glassfibre cowls in this particular photo.

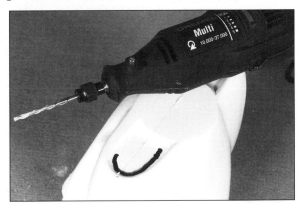

the power available is far greater coupled with the fact that it has a variable speed control. This gives you a speed range from 10 to 37000rpm which can be useful as the slower speeds are essential when working on plastics to avoid overheating. The higher speeds are useful when working on wood or metal with some of the many grinders, cutters, polishers, engravers, etc. available with the Dremel drill. An additional accessory with the Dremel is a three jaw chuck which enables you to use the finest drills right up to about 3mm, (⅛") diameter properly within this drill.

A recently introduced cutter is basically a drill tip which has cutting edges on the side, enabling you once you have pierced the material to move the drill in a sideways direction thereby converting it into a cutter. This would be very useful for cutting out air in-takes on glassfibre cowls but I am sure there are 101 other uses for it. The Dremel range is available direct from Microflame or the better model shops.

When you have cut out the various parts of your model and start on the assembly stage you will need to make sure that everything is square and lining up properly. There is a wide selection of adjustable and fixed squares available in the D-I-Y tool departments. The adjustable ones invariably have 90° and 45° settings on them but you can slide the ruler backwards and forwards adjusting the size to fit any situation.

Whilst you are building a model you will need to hold the parts together. I know that in a lot of situations, the parts will be pinned together whilst the glue dries but there will be other situations where clamping would be advisable. There are many small G clamps available which would be well worth looking at as different sizes will be required for different installations. Illustrated is a very small clamp which was actually made for tropical fish tank air systems. This is used to regulate the air supply from the pumps to these tanks but I have found many uses for it in modelling over the years so a visit to the pet shop might prove useful on this occasion! Wooden clothes pegs can also be very useful for holding components together whilst the glue is drying.

Very cheap 1" wide masking tape can also be used. This has the advantage that it can stuck anywhere and then peeled off without leaving any marks or damage to the wood when you have removed it.

When assembling a model some means of holding the parts together will be essential. Four types of "G" clamps are illustrated here. The simple wooden clothes peg can be very effective in many situations as well. In the foreground is a very small "G" clamp which is sold by pet shops for tropical fish tank application.

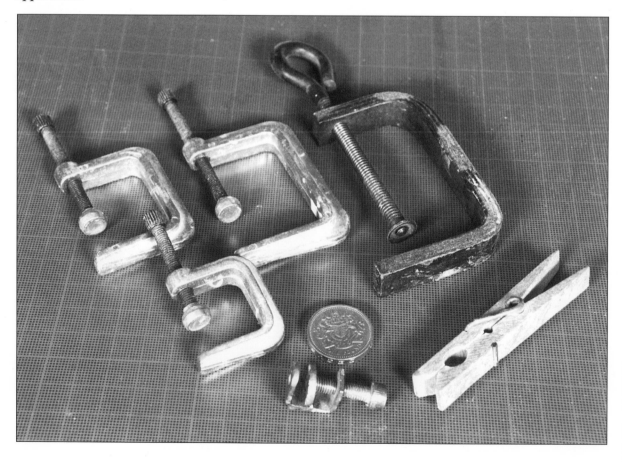

Notes

Other Titles

RADIO CONTROLLED MODEL AIRCRAFT BY ADRIAN VALE
£9.95 plus p&p
Adrian Vale's book on the basics of R/C Model Aircraft is an indispensable guide to getting started in flying model aeroplanes. The text is clear, down to earth and provides the best possible foundations for a successful career in flying model aircraft.

DESIGNING MODEL AIRCRAFT BY PETER MILLER
£7.95 plus p&p
Designing Model Aircraft covers everything you need to know about designing models, including aerodynamics and structural design. This book contains a complete guide to drawing, scaling plans up and flight testing your own model.

SCALE MODEL GLIDERS BY CLIFF CHARLESWORTH
£14.95 plus p&p
Cliff Charlesworth is one of the best known and well respected experts on scale gliding in the UK. In this book, he describes how to make a success of building and flying scale model gliders to the very highest standard up to and including competition level.

BASIC AERONAUTICS FOR MODELLERS BY ALASDAIR SUTHERLAND
£9.95 plus p&p
Alasdair Sutherland is a qualified aerodynamicist who is able to explain the theory and practice of model aeronautics in a way which everybody will understand. This book is essential reading for anyone who seriously considers themselves an informed modeller!

GAS TURBINE ENGINES FOR MODEL AIRCRAFT BY KURT SCHRECKLING
£14.95 plus p&p
For the first time Kurt Schreckling Strahlturbine Book is now available in English. It explains how to build Kurt Schreckling's turbojet motor, the FD3/64 containing full construction, photographs and working drawings.

MODEL JET ENGINES BY THOMAS KAMPS
£14.95 plus p&p
Following neatly on from Kurt Schreckling's book on the FD3/64, Thomas Kamps brings the construction and running of gas turbine engines up to date. The book includes highly detailed and well illustrated building instructions which the advanced model builder can use to make and even design his own jet engine.

GEARBOXES FOR ELECTRIC POWERED MODEL AIRCRAFT BY DIRK JURAS
£12.95 plus p&p
What is a gearbox and how do gearboxes work? Dirk Juras confronts those questions and the whole subject of gearboxes for electric model aircraft including guidelines on how to choose and match your gearbox, motor, propeller, installations and maintenance.

HIGH FLYING ON A LOW BUDGET BY PETER MILLER
£9.95 plus p&p
This book demonstrates in great detail that building and flying radio controlled model aircraft need not be prohibitively expensive. Covering everything from plans, low cost materials and where to find them, to making your own accessories and examining and buying second hand equipment.

MODEL ROCKETRY BY STUART LODGE
£12.95 plus p&p
Taking model rocketry past the basic kit stage and into the realms of sport models, high power rockets and competition space modelling. This is the most comprehensive book available today, covering the latest technological developments from around the world.

Traplet Publications Ltd., Traplet House, Severn Drive, Upton-upon-Severn, Worcestershire, WR8 0JL, England
Tel: +44 (0) 1684 594505 Fax: +44 (0) 1684 594586
E-mail: traplet@dial.pipex.com. Web Site: http://www.traplet.co.uk/traplet/